Gem Stones in Washington

Washington Geological Survey

with an introduction by Kerby Jackson

Introduction

It has been a century since the Department of Interior released it's important publication "Origin and Occurence of Gem Stones in Washington". First released in 1949, this important volume has been out of print and has been unavailable to the mining community since those days, with the exception of expensive original collector's copies and poorly produced digital editions.

It has often been said that "*gold is where you find it*", but even beginning prospectors understand that their chances for finding something of value in the earth or in the streams of the Golden West are dramatically increased by going back to those places where gold and other minerals were once mined by our forerunners. Despite this, much of the contemporary information on local mining history that is currently available is mostly a result of mere local folklore and persistent rumors of major strikes, the details and facts of which, have long been distorted. Long gone are the old timers and with them, the days of first hand knowledge of the mines of the area and how they operated. Also long gone are most of their notes, their assay reports, their mine maps and personal scrapbooks, along with most of the surveys and reports that were performed for them by private and government geologists. Even published books such as this one are often retired to the local landfill or backyard burn pile by the descendents of those old timers and disappear at an alarming rate. Despite the fact that we live in the so-called "Information Age" where information is supposedly only the push of a button on a keyboard away, true insight into mining properties remains illusive and hard to come by, even to those of us who seek out this sort of information as if our lives depend upon it. Without this type of information readily available to the average independent miner, there is little hope that our metal mining industry will ever recover.

This important volume and others like it, are being presented in their entirety again, in the hope that the average prospector will no longer stumble through the overgrown hills and the tailing strewn creeks without being well informed enough to have a chance to succeed at his ventures.

Kerby Jackson
Josephine County, Oregon
December 2014

CONTENTS

Page

Introduction 5

Gem-stone varieties of Washington 7
    Crystalline quartz 7
        Quartz crystal; rock crystal 7
        Amethyst; amethystine quartz 7
        Smoky quartz 7
        Milky quartz 7
    Chalcedonic quartz 7
        Agate; chalcedony 7
        Bloodstone 8
        Carnelian; sard 8
        Chert 8
        Flint 8
        Jasper 8
        Spherulitic jasper 8
        Prase 9
        Plasma 9
        Onyx 9
        Sardonyx 9
    Opal 9
        Common opal 9
        Hyalite 9
        Precious opal 9
        Fire opal 9
    Petrified wood 9
        Silicified wood 9
        Opalized wood 9

Origin of agate, jasper, and petrified wood 10
    Mineral-bearing solutions 10
    Cavities and cavity filling 11
    Color characteristics 13
    Release and removal from host rocks 14

Regions of the state and their collecting possibilities ... 15
    Northeastern region 15
    Southeastern region 15
    Northern Cascade Mountains and Puget Sound region 15
    Southern Cascade Mountains region 16
    Olympic Peninsula 16
    Southwestern region 17

Gem-stone localities of Washington 18
    Chelan County 18
    Clallam County 18
    Clark County 19
    Cowlitz County 20
    Douglas County 20
    Ferry County 20

		Page
Franklin County		20
Grant County		21
Grays Harbor County		21
Jefferson County		22
King County		22
Kittitas County		23
Klickitat County		25
Lewis County		25
Lincoln County		27
Mason County		27
Okanogan County		27
Pacific County		27
Pend Oreille County		28
Pierce County		28
San Juan County		28
Skagit County		29
Skamania County		29
Snohomish County		29
Stevens County		30
Thurston County		30
Whitman County		30
Yakima County		31

ORIGIN AND OCCURRENCE OF GEM STONES IN WASHINGTON

By Sheldon L. Glover

INTRODUCTION

Precious and semi-precious gem stones have fascinated mankind since before the dawn of history. As symbols of wealth and importance, they have appealed to all who could acquire them. Because of rarity that gives high value, they have been worn as a visible expression of affluence and hoarded as an easily portable and convertible medium of exchange. But more fundamental than rarity in the universal appeal of gem stones is their beauty—an outstanding inherent property—and the facility with which they lend themselves to personal adornment.

Unfortunately, the intrinsic value of true gem stones restricts their accumulation to the wealthy. The average person can afford none at all, or, at most, only one or two, and so is unable to build up a collection of individual stones. Nevertheless, the urge to collect beautiful stones has persisted and, in recent years, has led to the realization by an ever-increasing number of everyday people that semi-precious and non-precious, yet highly attractive, agates, petrified wood, and other available mineral substances may be substituted for costly gems with an astonishing feeling of personal satisfaction.

Now that transportation is so simplified and good roads make nearly all regions accessible, the recreational pursuit of attractive gem-stone material is within the reach of all. Then, too, equipment for cutting and polishing has become more-or-less standardized and does not entail a prohibitive outlay of money, making it possible for anyone to transform rough agates and kindred materials into objects of beauty. As a hobby, there are few activities that so satisfy the basic desire to collect numbers of similar or related items under healthful outdoor conditions and at such slight expense. As a result, agate and mineral societies and clubs have been organized in most of the larger centers of population, so groups bound by a common interest can meet, exhibit their finds and collections, and discuss gathering areas and polishing techniques. Thirteen of these societies or clubs are now active in Washington; the membership of each ranges from about 25 to nearly 200 and in aggregate amounts to nearly 1,000 persons.

The growth of the hobby is indicated by the increasing number of letters received by the Division of Mines and Geology asking for information on collecting areas. As adequate response to inquiries cannot be made through correspondence, it was decided to prepare this report, gathering together all data on gem-stone occurrences that are in the files of the Division and including the personal observations made by the writer during the more than 30 years in which he has been interested in the subject. An effort has been made to avoid the use of technical terms so far as possible, but it is presumed that the reader either has or can obtain some basic knowledge of geology and mineralogy. Many easily understood texts are available in the public libraries or by purchase for those lacking an elementary knowledge of geology.

The subject of general mineral collecting is not considered here. Washington is well supplied with a large variety of metallic and nonmetallic minerals, and many enthusiasts get a great deal of pleasure out of collecting these materials. The mines and prospects of the state form the hunting ground for those who have this hobby, and many reports by the Division of Mines and Geology are available to them. Heretofore, however, no comprehensive report has been available to the usual collector interested in agate, jasper, petrified wood, and the few other mineral substances occurring in Washington—all classed, somewhat questionably, as gem stones. The present report is published in an effort to, in part at least, overcome this lack. It is realized that the list of localities where materials have been or can be collected is far from complete. Probably the members of the agate and mineral societies know of many places worth visiting in addition to those mentioned here. If these people will cooperate with the Division of Mines and Geology to the extent of supplying information on collecting localities, it may be possible to greatly improve this report in some future edition.

GEM-STONE VARIETIES OF WASHINGTON

Gem stones have acquired a host of names—some distinctive and useful, some confusing and needless. Schaller[1] has compiled a list of these, showing 867 names that have been applied to 119 mineral substances. He enumerates 193 separate names that have been given to the one mineral quartz—some, because the need for variety designation is indicated by a distinct variation in physical or optical properties, but the most, as a result of someone's whim or eccentricity. Similarly, 53 names are listed for the mineral garnet—some being desirable, as they indicate distinct varieties, and some, arbitrary and senseless. No useful purpose would be served here by enumerating the great variety of gem stones or by including detailed mineralogical descriptions of them. In the first place, only a few are known to occur in Washington and this account is concerned only with them; and secondly, because excellent mineralogies and other reference books are available in public libraries or through purchase for anyone desiring further information.

A collector working in Washington should be familiar with the following mineral substances.[2] Chemically, these are all more-or-less common varieties of silica—the element silicon combined with oxygen as silicon dioxide, SiO_2.

CRYSTALLINE QUARTZ

Quartz crystal; rock crystal.—Ordinary quartz, clear, colorless, or nearly so, occurring as individual crystals or as clumps of crystals, usually terminating in 6-sided pyramids when unbroken.

Amethyst; amethystine quartz.—Crystalline quartz having a clear purple or bluish-violet color, usually best shown near the crystal terminations.

Smoky quartz.—Crystalline quartz, usually clear, having a smoky-yellow to dark smoky-brown color.

Milky quartz.—Crystalline quartz, translucent to opaque, of milky white color. It commonly occurs as vein material and may contain gold and other metallic minerals.

CHALCEDONIC QUARTZ

Agate; chalcedony.—An extremely fine-grained or dense variety of translucent quartz that does not show crystal form (cryptocrystalline), which has a somewhat waxy luster, and which may occur in a considerable variety of colors. Many of the color variants of chalcedony have long had individual names. In ordinary usage *chalcedony* and *agate* are practically synonymous. Possibly, the

---

[1] Schaller, W. T., Gem names: U. S. Geol. Survey Mineral Resources for 1917, pp. 147-168, 1920.

[2] See also Dana, E. S., and Ford, W. E., a textbook of mineralogy: John Wiley & Sons, Inc., New York, 1932, or other standard texts and reference books.

term chalcedony implies a certain origin (a cavity filling) as well as a definite mineralogical composition and nature; while the term agate has come to have a more general connotation, implying only composition. Theoretically, chalcedony is of uniform color and agate is irregularly colored, usually in more-or-less wavy layers, a distinction that is not generally applied and which is not made in this report.

Bloodstone.—Similar to plasma but containing small inclusions of red jasper.

Carnelian; sard.—A clear red or brownish-red to brown chalcedony, pale to deep in shade.

Chert.—A dull, opaque dense quartzose rock occurring in various rather light colors. It is somewhat like chalcedony but is more impure and, usually, unattractive in appearance.

Flint.—A dark-gray, brown, or black extremely dense form of chert, commonly altered to white or light gray on the surface of nodules.

Jasper.—Ordinary jasper is a dense opaque siliceous rock having a uniform red color. Less commonly, it occurs in shades of yellow, brown, or even dark green, but always with an opacity that is characteristic. It seems unfortunate that the term jasper is not restricted to the red variety, for that is the color that is usually thought of when the material is mentioned. Some typical jaspers result from the crystallization of solutions of silica in which a sufficient amount of either finely divided or flocculent iron oxide is present to give the resultant quartzose mass the characteristic (usually red) color. Other jaspers, probably equally typical, result from the solidification to chalcedony (without crystallization) of similar iron-rich siliceous solutions. The most attractive specimens are those in which the red iron oxide is present in insufficient amount to entirely color the rock but appears as clots and irregular flocculent masses and swirls in a matrix that may be either translucent finely crystalline quartz or chalcedony. Brecciated red jasper is sometimes cemented by chalcedony or chert.

Spherulitic jasper.—The usual Washington form is an aggregate of red jasper spherulites, ranging in size from 1/2 millimeter to 4 millimeters in diameter, in a dark-brown to black matrix. The spherulites in some instances show concentric layering (a concretionary or oölotic structure) in contrasting shades of red, but this feature is not so obvious when a thin section is viewed under a petrographic microscope; then a radiating structure is apparent. Rarely, the spherulites have a center of crystalline quartz surrounded by yellow jasper which in turn is surrounded by red jasper. The individual spherulites are commonly cracked in a star pattern which has later been filled with colorless chalcedony. The matrix in which the spherulites are embedded is a yellow to nearly colorless chalcedony so filled with dust-like particles of a metallic oxide (chiefly of iron and a minor amount of manganese) that it is opaque and shows a blue-black metallic luster to the unaided eye.

The spherulitic jasper of Washington is very similar to that of California which occurs in the San Francisco Bay region and was named and well described by W. T. Schaller of the U. S. Geological Survey.[1] Unfortunately, amateur mineralogists have applied the misnomer "orbicular jasper" to this material, a term that has now come into rather common use but which is entirely inapplicable and should be avoided. Orbicular is a term correctly applied to a peculiar mineralogic structural feature of granitic rocks,[2] while spherultic is properly a textural or structural term used to describe a certain feature of inorganic chemically deposited sediments such as chert, flint, and jasper.[3]

Prase.—Translucent to dull leek-green chalcedony.

Plasma.—Bright-green to dark grass-green subtranslucent or feebly translucent chalcedony.

Onyx.—Chalcedony in even, plane layers of contrasting color.

Sardonyx.—Onyx that has included layers of carnelian.

OPAL

Opal is an amorphous or colloidal form of silica (SiO_2) chemically combined with a small amount of water. It is not quite as hard as quartz and has a lower specific gravity.

Common opal.—A translucent to subtranslucent form of ordinary opal lacking "fire" or play of colors and occurring in various colors such as: white (milk opal), yellow, brown, red, green, and black.

Hyalite.—A transparent, colorless variety of common opal.

Precious opal.—A transparent to translucent variety of opal that exhibits a delicate play of colors.

Fire opal.—Precious opal showing fire-like flashes of color.

PETRIFIED WOOD

Silicified wood.—A replacement of wood by silica (quartz). The grain of the original wood is usually preserved.

Opalized wood.—A replacement of wood by opal, generally of the common variety. The original grain is usually preserved, but in some instances it is obliterated.

[1] In Sterrett, D. B., Gems and precious stones: U. S. Geol. Survey Mineral Resources for 1910, pp. 870, 871, 1911.

[2] Johannsen, Albert, A descriptive petrography of the igneous rocks, vol. 2, pp. 248-259, 349-354, 387-388, Chicago, Ill., University of Chicago Press, 1932.

[3] Twenhofel, W. H., Principles of sedimentation, pp. 367-379, 570. New York, McGraw-Hill Book Co., 1939.

ORIGIN OF AGATE, JASPER, AND PETRIFIED WOOD

Washington is far less favored than are some states, for example Oregon and Montana, in the occurrence of agate and other materials of interest to the collector. Yet it is possible to find agate, jasper, silicified and opalized wood, and many other colorful materials in certain areas and, in favorable places there, in considerable quantity. Some consideration of the conditions under which these substances form and occur and of the applicable geology of the state adds interest to collecting and doubtlessly would increase the efficiency of the collector in pursuing his hobby. As the three most popular collector's items are agate, jasper, and opalized wood, the origin of these materials warrants attention.

MINERAL-BEARING SOLUTIONS

Water exists at most places at a greater or lesser depth in the ground; it may occur in the loose surficial deposits overlying the bedrock and to considerable depth in the bedrock itself. This is known as "ground water"; it is tapped for domestic and industrial use by dug or drilled wells and appears as springs where conditions are favorable. Ground water is seldom static, or free from movement; usually it slowly percolates through the strata under the influence of gravity. In its travel it dissolves and picks up mineral matter from the rocks through which it moves. Depending on the kind and solubility of the minerals composing the rock, the ground water may become feebly to strongly charged with various compounds of calcium ("lime"), sodium, iron, or many other elements. One compound that may be present in solution in this way is silica.

Water is also a component of molten igneous rocks, particularly those of the more acid (siliceous) varieties. Common examples of such rocks, when cooled, are granite and rhyolite. This hot so-called "magmatic" water has a strong dissolving action on the silicate minerals composing the rocks through which it travels. As the silicates are decomposed, silica is released, to be carried in probably a colloidal form by the water. The water may finally issue as a hot spring, as is common in regions of recent volcanic activity, or it may join and become a part of the ordinary ground water of the region.

Just as water, in working its way slowly through the rock of the earth's surface, dissolves and carries silica when conditions are favorable for such action, so it releases and deposits silica when conditions change to those favoring deposition. This change may be a variation in the chemical nature of the rock traversed, or the change may be to a lower pressure or temperature, or to some other conditions differing from those formerly prevailing. When the deposition of silica does occur it takes place in pore spaces and voids in the rock or other material that the solution happens to be in. In this way it may impregnate and "silicify" permeable rocks; it may replace, molecule by molecule, the cells of deeply buried vegetal or other organic matter, thus causing "petrifaction"; or it may fill cracks and cavities that exist in the host rock. The collector is chiefly interested in petrifaction, whereby wood is silicified or opalized, and in cavity filling, whereby agates and related stones come into existence.

CAVITIES AND CAVITY FILLING

Open cavities in which silica-bearing solutions could deposit chalcedony were rare in some of the rock varieties that make up the bedrock of the state and fairly abundant in other varieties. Knowing this, one can predict in what formations agates and related cavity fillings may be expected and where the chances are against their occurrence.

Cavities were rare in the sedimentary rocks of Washington. In some states, notably Iowa, cavities are thought to have formed in some sedimentary beds through the removal of soluble ("limy") concretionary nodules, the empty spaces later to be filled by chalcedony or other minerals; so far as known, no instance of this process has been found in Washington. Cavities were rare, too, in metamorphic rocks and in almost all igneous rocks except those extrusive, volcanic varities known as rhyolite, andesite, and basalt. The metamorphoric rocks and the intrusive igneous rocks, such as granite, commonly show breaks that resulted from jointing, fracturing, and faulting; in these, under favorable conditions, were formed quartz veins and associated deposits of ore minerals. Open cavities or "vugs" may have occurred in the quartz veins and in the ore deposits, representing remnants of original openings, solution cavities, or volatile constituents (of the ore solutions) that later disappeared. These vugs may be lined or filled with crystals of quartz, calcite (calcium carbonate), or various other minerals; however, fillings of agate and jasper are rare under such circumstances.

The most favorable rocks, therefore, are the extrusive, volcanic varieties. These, in their original molten state sometimes contained considerable gas or entrapped steam. In consequence, as they cooled under conditions of lessened pressure, holes and cavities in the shape of the expanded gas bubbles commonly developed. The size of cavities formed in this way, their distribution through the rock, and their abundance, of course vary greatly, depending on the amount of gas originally present, its distribution through the rock mass, and the viscosity of the originally molten material. They may be so numerous (particularly in basalt) as to make the rock cellular, or "vesicular," giving it a spongelike appearance due to the myriad of smoothly rounded spaces, ranging from the size of a pinhead to that of a large bean or almond. Under exceptional conditions, and then chiefly in the more acid rocks—andesite and particularly rhyolite—the holes or cavities may be relatively sparse but relatively large. Sizes comparable to those of oranges and grapefruit are common, and much larger cavities are formed occasionally. These, too, may be smoothly rounded, but it is far more usual for them to be irregular in outline, and sometimes they are collapsed to greatly elongated, relatively thin shapes.

Any such holes and cavities, in whatever kind of rock they occur, may be entirely empty; or they may be merely lined with some mineral, such as chalcedony, hyalite, or calcite. In such instances, either no mineral-bearing solution reached the cavities or an insufficient amount had access to the cavities to fill them. If the walls of a cavity are mineral-lined but the interior is empty, the result is a "geode." Great variations occur in these interesting forms. The wall lining may be very thin, or it may be so thick that but little space remains unoccupied. It may consist of but one mineral, or more than one mineral, or different varieties of a single mineral, depending on the nature of the solutions and on whether differing solutions were present at various times during the formation of the geode. For example: a common form of geode has an outer shell (the initial cavity lining) of chalcedony and, attached to and merging into it, an inner layer of crystalline quartz.

When the time for filling was adequate and the available minerals in solution were sufficient to entirely fill the cavity, the deposited mineral matter became a solid mass. The resultant nodule may show that it formed just as a geode does, in concentric, usually wavy, layers of one or more minerals separately deposited, or, more commonly, of different forms of the same mineral—for instance, chalcedonic and crystalline quartz, or variously colored forms of chalcedony. On the other hand, it may be obvious in some instances that the filling did not deposit as a lining on the more-or-less spherical walls of the cavity but rather as a gradual horizontal accumulation, sometimes layer upon layer, from the bottom to the top. In fact, the deposition of chalcedony as a complete wall lining (which, if the process had stopped, would have resulted in a geode) may have been followed by a final horizontal filling of what remained of the original cavity, giving horizontally banded agate surrounded by curved layers of the same material. Great variety exists in agate nodules, but the general process of formation of all is essentially the same.

Occurences of vesicular basalt are very common in southeastern and also in some parts of southwestern Washington. They may be seen in road cuts and quarries and in many other excavations where the bedrock is lava. In most instances, these small cavities or vesicles are either entirely devoid of mineral filling or have only a thin lining on their walls. In other places, the spaces are completely filled with zeolites (chiefly complex hydrous calcium silicates), calcite, or, occasionally, chalcedony or even opal; then the rock is said to be "amygdaloidal" and the fillings are called "amygdules." In instances most commonly met with, amygdules are too small or too unattractive to interest the collector, and it is the larger, unfortunately rarer, cavity filling formed sometimes in basalt and more commonly in andesite and particularly in rhyolite that is sought for.

COLOR CHARACTERISTICS

The variations in color shown by chalcedony and other quartz varieties are generally considered to be due to minute amounts of various elements present as impurities. Thus, pure quartz is water-clear and colorless; some chalcedonies are also clear or they may be snow-white. Commonly, chalcedony is delicately to strongly colored yellow, brown, or red, owing to the presence of lesser or greater amounts of iron. Still other colors are green (from a trace of nickel or chromium); blue (probably from an iron compound); and black (probably from some organic material).

These coloring agents may have been present in the original silica-bearing solutions, so attractive stones were formed. In many instances, however, the solutions were relatively free from coloring matter and therefore produced unattractive nearly colorless, gray, or slightly yellowish agate nodules. Fortunately for the collector, during the ages that many of these drab agates have been buried since their original formation, they have been subject to the coloring effects of later mineral-bearing solutions; hence have absorbed coloring agents and have acquired attractive colors they did not originally possess. When colored subsequent to formation, the hue may be only a surface effect, or it may penetrate the stone to a considerable depth, or it may selectively color certain permeable layers of the agate in striking contrast to less permeable layers. Incidentally, advantage is sometimes taken of the variations in relative permeability of the different layers composing agates to color them artificially to spectacular hues; large Brazilian agates, occasionally seen in museums and in private collections, usually owe their brilliant contrasting color bands to this "gilding of the lily." Possibly the end justifies the means, as beautiful specimens result.

Opalized wood, common in various parts of eastern Washington, was colored when formed or later, in the same way that agates are. The petrifaction was an infinitely slow process. When the wood cells were replaced throughout by silica having essentially the same coloring trace-elements, a uniform color resulted. When the process was occasionally interrupted, so that part of the vegetal matter was replaced at one time and part at another, allowing time for changes in solution composition, a variegation in color and shades resulted.

The red of common jasper is due to ferric oxide included in considerable amount in a chalcedony or quartz matrix. The more desirable jaspers variously known as variegated, "Egyptian," agate, and "calico" have clots and formless, flocculent masses of ferric oxide distributed at random through a chalcedony or quartz matrix that may be green, yellow, or translucent in delicate tints.

RELEASE AND REMOVAL FROM HOST ROCKS

Whenever rock is exposed to the atmosphere, weathering takes place. By this means the rock, over a long period of time, disintegrates, decomposes and softens, and even may become clay. Cavity fillings may be harder and more resistant to weathering than the original rock and so remain hard and unaltered when the host rock is completely decomposed. This is particularly true of chalcedonic fillings. In consequence, geodes, amygules, and agate nodules may be found as loose stones in a clay or grit, the residual material from what was originally a lava flow. It is more common, however, for erosion to carry away the residual products of rock decay, in which case the agate materials are also removed from their place of origin to finally come to rest in the gravels of ancient or modern stream beds and beaches.

It is relatively uncommon in Washington to find loose agate masses or nodules in the original shape and condition in which they were formed, even though they lie in a residual clay derived in place from the decomposition of the host rock. Usually the nodules have become fractured by stresses that affected the host rock at some time in its history, or they have been broken by frost action or have suffered other mechanical damage. Alluvial agates—those that have been transported by streams—are almost invariably angular, subangular, or rounded fragments of the original masses or nodules.

Under certain conditions of moderate erosion, it is possible for the agate nodules, together with similarly hard material from sedimentary beds that may have been associated with the old lava flows, to become concentrated on surfaces of gentle slope, while finer material of less weight is carried farther away. Concentrations of this kind exist on the bedrock surface of parts of southwestern Washington; for example, in the vicinity of Tono, Thurston County. However, sedimentary beds of sand and clay have commonly been deposited at a later time and so conceal the agate accumulations. This cover is relatively thin in some places, so there it is possible to dig down to the bedrock and discover any agates, jasper, and petrified wood that may lie on it.

REGIONS OF THE STATE AND THEIR COLLECTING POSSIBILITIES

When the foregoing considerations are applied to the regional geology of the state it becomes possible to estimate the possibilities of various areas as sources of agates and related materials. That an occasional agate is found in an unfavorable area, and that persistent search may fail to produce agates in a favorable area, are quite understandable. In the first instance, it is possible for chalcedonic material to form under quite adverse conditions. Then, too, glaciers and streams may carry agates from a distant source and leave them in places where their occurrence would not be expected. In the second instance, prolonged collecting may have depleted the occurrences in a favorable locality, the stones may be concealed by barren deposits or vegetation, or, despite appearances, the local conditions may not be as favorable as assumed.

NORTHEASTERN REGION

In a general way, the areas of granite and related rocks and of metamorphic rocks, common in the northern row of counties from the Cascade Mountains to the Idaho line, are not particularly favorable for the occurrence of agates, jasper, or petrified wood. However, in this region quartz veins are abundant, so milky quartz is of common occurrence, and occasionally quartz crystal and amethyst are found. The most attractive crystalline quartz is usually in vugs occurring in ore deposits and in various rock formations; their presence is entirely fortuitous and cannot be predicted.

SOUTHEASTERN REGION

That part of eastern Washington south of the northern row of counties and east of the Cascade Mountains is almost entirely underlain by the Columbia basalt flows. This rock, in the upper part of individual flows, is commonly vesicular and in some places is amygdaloidal, but, with a very few notable exceptions, mentioned later, it is mostly barren of material that is attractive to the collector. Interbedded with the lava in numerous places are beds of sand, "ashy" sands, and silty clays that commonly contain opalized wood. Occasionally, opalized wood, ranging in size from small fragments to nearly whole logs, is found where the wood was originally entrapped in the flows themselves, or between flows where little if any sedimentary material occurs. Also, later sedimentary deposits lying on top of the basalt bedrock are rather abundantly agatiferous in certain places, the chalcedonic material having originated an unknown distance away to be transported by ancient streams onto the lava plains.

NORTHERN CASCADE MOUNTAINS AND PUGET SOUND REGION

Conditions in the northern Cascade Mountains and extending approximately to the south boundaries of King County on the west and Chelan County on the east are relatively unfavorable, though isolated agates are sometimes found, and some petrified wood and jasper occur in the Swauk sedimentary beds that extend northwestward from Wenatchee. Quartz veins are as abundant here as in the northeastern region, and mining or prospecting operations sometimes disclose quartz-crystal-filled vugs.

Occasional agates, jaspers, and pieces of petrified wood are found in the glacial deposits adjacent to Puget Sound, but they are relatively rare. The chance of finding interesting material is better on the beaches of the Sound, Admiralty Inlet, Hood Canal, and Strait of Juan de Fuca, for here gravels in endless amount are well exposed to the collector and favorable conditions exist for the harder, siliceous materials to be concentrated. As a result, these beaches continually yield a few agates to persistent search, but these are mostly small, of poor color, and too sparse to repay the time spent in their collection.

SOUTHERN CASCADE MOUNTAINS REGION

The southern Cascade Mountains region, together with the adjoining lowlands on either side, from King and Chelan Counties on the north to the Columbia River on the south, is relatively favorable for the occurrence of agates and related materials. Basalt is a common rock here, and much of this must have originally contained an unusual amount of water vapor or other gases, for voids of considerable size were formed in many places when the flows cooled. Andesite is an abundant rock throughout the region. Rhyolite underlies areas of considerable size in Kittitas and Pierce Counties and is associated with andesite in various places in other parts of the region. Chalcedony formed in rather large amounts in some of these rocks, so that it and related materials may now be found where weathering and erosion have released the nodules from the host rocks. Some of the material is in place, or nearly so, and occurs in residual clays and in disintegrated outcrops. Much of it, however, has been carried by streams a considerable distance from its place of formation.

Although this region, in general, is probably the best in the state from a collector's viewpoint, it does not contain any such excellent agate localities as are found, for example, in Oregon and Montana. One area here that is deserving of attention is along Swauk Creek and the Teanaway River in Kittitas County, the tributaries of these streams, and the adjacent hilly to mountainous terrain. Another area, less well defined, is along the west slope of the Cascade Mountains and in the adjacent foothills and lowlands from Tenino to Vancouver.

OLYMPIC PENINSULA

The Olympic Peninsula is somewhat more favorable than the northern Cascade Mountain area, though agates and petrified wood seldom occur either in the sedimentary rocks that compose most of the region or in the basaltic rocks that form a horseshoe-shaped belt around the north, east, and south sides of the peninsula. However, these basalts in some places have "ellipsoidal" or pillowlike forms that were developed when they originally cooled as a result of being extruded into shallow water, and the spaces between the individual "pillows" and of the natural shrinkage cracks and joints of the rock are commonly filled with later mineral matter. The most usual filling materials are a siliceous limestone and a more-or-less calcareous chert; the latter may be white or variously colored by iron and manganese to shades of yellow, brown, pink, purple, and red. In general, it lacks translucency, brightness, and clearness of color, but some specimens have an interesting appearance. Another and far less common filling is jasper. This may be the usual red, but variegated and spherulitic varieties occur. Finding these more attractive materials in place within the area where volcanic rocks crop out is not impossible though it is very difficult. A better procedure is to search for pebbles and boulders of transported jasper in stream gravels of the area and along the ocean beaches to the west. Beach gravels from Grays Harbor north to Cape Flattery are quite productive, the best accumulations being probably in the La Push-Cape Johnson vicinity.

SOUTHWESTERN REGION

The Willapa Hills region of southwestern Washington (south of Grays Harbor) has an abundance of basaltic rock formations but lacks the more acid volcanic rock with which agates are usually associated. The agates found there along the beaches and streams— never abundantly—are mostly in, or are washed from, the unconsolidated Pleistocene sands and gravels that overlie the earlier bedrock. They originated far to the east and were transported into the area by streams during the time the glacial ice was present in the Puget Sound region. In some places a thin, sparse stratum of hard, siliceous pebbles and cobbles lies on the bedrock at the base of the Pleistocene beds; in this, agates, petrified wood, and jasper may usually be found. Fossilized marine shells (most commonly, forms similar to clams and snails) are abundant in some of the sedimentary rocks of the area. These sometimes have a chalcedonic filling and make interesting collector's items.

GEM-STONE LOCALITIES OF WASHINGTON

To obtain precise locations where agates and related materials have been found or where collections can be made is usually rather difficult. It may be done in some instances, but commonly the available information is based on hearsay, rumor, and unsubstantiated reports. Occasionally there is no question of a considerable number of agates having been found at some place, but the finder may have only a confused idea of where this is. If the find was recent, he could probably retrace his steps, but he may not be able to describe to another person the route followed. In western Washington particularly, explicit directions are needed because of concealing vegetation. All this may add zest to the search; certainly a well-deserved feeling of accomplishment attends the finding of an agate locality by following the usual indefinite directions. The best procedure is to accompany agate-club members or other individuals who have accidentally or through trial and error learned how to reach promising localities.

In the following pages, under county headings, is given information on the materials of most general interest to collectors and the best available data on their location. Some of the place designations are vague indeed, but people living in the vicinity may be able to supply further details.

CHELAN COUNTY

AGATES

Davenport property.—In secs. 7 and 8, T. 22 N., R. 17 E., on the north side of Negro Creek. It is reported that agate-lined geodes, whole and broken, have been found in this vicinity. No details are available.

MEXICAN, OR TRAVERTINE, ONYX

Blewett Pass.—The variety of calcium carbonate rock known as Mexican, or travertine, onyx, in blue, black, and buff colors, is reported to have been found cropping out at the top of a ridge 2 or 3 miles east (?) of the Blewett Pass summit. Other details are unknown.

QUARTZ CRYSTAL

Crown Point mine.—This is in the SE¼ sec. 8, T. 31 N., R. 16 E. at the head of the cirque west of Lyman Lake. An adit in diorite, 200 feet below the molybdenite vein, exposes a vuggy zone containing quartz crystals as much as 2 inches in length.

CLALLAM COUNTY

AGATES

Agate Bay or Agate Beach.—On the Strait of Juan de Fuca, just west of Crescent Bay, in T. 31 N., R. 8 W. Formerly, agates were plentiful enough here to give the name to the bay or beach. They occur occasionally in the gravel of beaches all along the Strait, having come out of the transported gravel of the glacial drift that is abundant in the region. In the Crescent Bay area, however, it is possible that some additional agates have weathered out of the basalt which crops out in this vicinity.

(See also Grays Harbor County.)

JASPER

Ed. B. manganese claims.—West of Lake Crescent, 6½ miles airline, in the SE¼ of sec. 24, T. 30 N., R. 11 W. Ellipsoidal basalt is exposed in the gully occupied by Eureka Creek. In the creek bed near the tunnel of the Ed. B. group of manganese claims, spherulitic jasper in masses as much as 6 inches across forms the filling between the individual basalt pillows.

Lake Crescent.—A huge boulder of spherulitic jasper, weighing several tons, was found in a gully at about 2,000 feet in altitude approximately a mile northwest of the west end of Lake Crescent. This is between the Daisy and Peggy manganese claims. Some individual spherulites showed white and yellow centers in addition to the more common red varieties.

Ocean coast.—To the north and south of the mouth of the Quillayutte River (at La Push), particularly in the 2 miles of gravelly and bouldery beach north of the river and Rialto Beach, spherulitic jasper, plain jasper, and occasionally chalcedonic jasper of various kinds occur in considerable quantity as pebbles and cobbles. These materials may be found, also, in other gravelly beaches up and down the coast, as in the vicinity of Kalaloch, Jefferson County, but vagaries of the ocean current expose new gravels in one place while concealing gravels at another place, so gathering localities change from year to year.

Other localities.—Spherulitic jasper has been brought to the Division of Mines and Geology by Olympic Peninsula manganese prospectors but without locations being designated. It has been found as float on the Dungeness and Soleduck Rivers, indicating that the material is not uncommon within the belt of basaltic extrusive rocks with which the manganese is associated.[1] Variously colored chert also occurs in some places associated with ellipsoidal basalt, as near Staircase on the Skykomish River just above Lake Cushman.

CLARK COUNTY
(See Cowlitz County.)

---

[1] Green, S. H., Manganese deposits of the Olympic Peninsula, Washington: Washington Div. Mines and Mining Rept. of Inv. No. 7, 1945.

COWLITZ COUNTY
AGATES, GEODES, AND JASPER

Silver Lake locality.—East of the lake from the west quarter corner of sec. 8, T. 9 N., R. 1 E., northward and eastward along the railroad grade of the Weyerhaeuser Timber Co.; also along the road running northwest from the south center of sec. 8 and crossing the railroad grade in the SW¼ sec. 5. A perfect clear-quartz-lined geode, 4 inches across, was found by the writer in residual clay of the railroad cut just northeast of the road crossing, and fragments of geodes are common throughout the area. Most of the material is chalcedonic and of a poor gray to light-buff color; but better-colored material, together with highly colored jasperized wood, is reported to occur in the soil overlying "hardpan" at a depth of 6 to 24 inches in the W½ sec. 5.

Other localities.—The part of Cowlitz County 15 or 20 miles east of the Cowlitz River and extending from the north county line south to and possibly beyond the Lewis River is favorable for the occurrence of agates and related materials. Collections have been made in the hills east of Kalama and Kelso, and the whole region is deserving of attention. The Kalama area is particularly noted for the interesting zeolite fillings of a vesicular and vuggy basalt, in places considerably altered and softened, that forms the bedrock of the region. An abundance of excellent specimen material has been collected here.

DOUGLAS COUNTY

Moses Coulee.—Precious opal has been reported from Moses Coulee, but the occurrence could not be verified. It is reasonable to expect opal to be present somewhere there as amygdules in the great basalt outcrops of the coulee walls. Kunz' statement regarding Douglas County,[1] that "a rich golden semiopal of great beauty is found, also red, olive-green, and striking minglings of all three colors" probably refers to occurrences of opalized wood. He gives no location details.

FERRY COUNTY
AMETHYST

It is reported that amethystine quartz occurs 15 miles northeast of Republic. Further details are lacking, but miners and prospectors of the vicinity could probably supply information.

FRANKLIN COUNTY
AGATES

White Bluffs locality.—On the east side of the Columbia River, 16 miles upriver from Pasco, from Byers Landing to Ringold.[2] A

---

[1] Kunz, G. F., Precious stones: U. S. Geol. Survey 17th Ann. Rept., pt. 3, p. 915, 1896.
[2] U. S. Geol. Survey Pasco quadrangle topographic map.

stratigraphic thickness of about 150 feet of iron-stained gravels and cobbles crops out in the river banks and bluffs at the base of the White Bluffs (Ringold) exposures. The gravels are well-rounded and stream-worn. They consist of a great variety of rock types, among which quartzite is particularly abundant and agate and jasper are of frequent occurrence. The agates are chiefly gray and buff-colored chalcedony, but some have attractive red hues. Some of the jasper forms a matrix for an unusual breccia of white to cream-colored quartzite. The best collecting is in the draws and gullies and on the intervening spurs, where erosion has cleaned concealing coatings from the stones.

GRANT COUNTY
OPALIZED WOOD

Saddle Mountain.—Considerable opalized wood occurs between Othello and Beverly, in the Saddle Mountain area. Some relatively large parts of logs have been found, producing material of excellent color. Advantage can be taken here of deep excavations provided by canyons and gullies cut into the basalt and interbasalt sediments. Flake wood in the wash at the foot of a gully serves to indicate prospecting sites up the gully.

CHALCEDONY

Moses Lake vicinity.—Cores from a deep oil-test well in the northwest corner of sec. 19, T. 17 N., R. 28 E. showed a vesicular basalt at a depth of 3,850 feet in which occurred blue chalcedonic amygdules the size of one's thumb. Of course, these are inaccessible to a collector, but they indicate some possibilities in the outcropping basalt of the region.

GRAYS HARBOR COUNTY
AGATES

Ocean coast.—Agates are sometimes found in the beach gravels of the west coast of the Olympic Peninsula but they are not common. Many years ago, before collectors had so thoroughly worked the beaches, they were more numerous and some large collections of attractively colored material were made. One beach area that, 40 years ago, produced excellent red agates was from Copalis to Point Grenville.

The writer has found several ovoid frosted pebbles, the size of one's thumb, worn from single water-clear quartz crystals, in beach gravels immediately adjacent to the north side of Point Grenville.

SILICIFIED WOOD

Silicified wood, generally quite unattractive, weathers out of various formations of the Peninsula region and may be found as pebbles and boulders in stream and beach gravels. Specimens showing fossilized teredo borings are sometimes found. Considerable wood occurs in the Quinault formation of Cape Elizabeth. Mostly, this is not petrified, but one unusual 6-inch log, 8 feet long, was found by the writer where wave action had partly eroded the enclosing sandstone. Part of this log was entirely silicified, part was carbonized and coaly, and part was a still unaltered, though darkened, wood from which shavings could be cut. A whittled piece of the wood gradually darkened to jet-black within a period of 3 months; it was then hard and susceptible to a high polish.

JASPER

Plain jasper is not uncommon in the gravels of streams flowing from the Olympic Mountains. Aside from the spherulitic variety (see Clallam County), this material is of but little interest to most collectors.

OTHER COLLECTOR'S ITEMS

Pyrite concretions, 1 to 2 inches in diameter, weather from shale cropping out along the ocean bluff near a small creek three-fourths of a mile south of the mouth of Raft River and also in a similar situation about half a mile south of Little Hogs Back, in the NW¼ sec. 4, T. 22 N., R. 13 W. The abundance varies greatly from time to time, but usually it is possible to collect large numbers of smoothly rounded to subangular masses of solid pyrite, surface oxidized to a brown color, from gravel accumulations of the upper beach.

JEFFERSON COUNTY

(See also Clallam and Grays Harbor Counties.)

QUARTZ CRYSTAL

Mount Anderson.—It is reported that clear quartz crystals as much as 2 inches in length are quite numerous in the NW¼SW¼ sec. 28, T. 26 N., R. 5 W. No further details are available.

Rustler Creek.—Quartz crystals 2 inches long and from 1 to 1½ inches in diameter are reported to occur in vuggy parts of a quartz vein that crops out in the SW¼SW¼ sec. 31, T. 25 N., R. 7 W.

KING COUNTY
QUARTZ CRYSTAL

Denny Mountain.—A thick bed of limestone crops out on the southwest side of Denny Mountain, above Denny Creek, about 1½ miles west of Snoqualmie Pass. This is in the W½NW¼ sec. 5 and the E½NE¼ sec. 6, T. 22 N., R. 11 E. At the northwest end of the main limestone body the writer found a loose slab of bluish-gray chalcedony, a foot or so across, covered with a stand of large clear quartz crystals. It obviously came from no great distance above the limestone outcrop. Incidentally, massive garnet, unattractive, so far as observed, forms an irregular body 10 feet or more in width along the northeast side of the limestone; gray calcite crystals, many feet across, have formed from the recrystallization of the limestone at the upper northwest end of the limestone body; and large glittering crystals of specularite (micaceous hematite, an iron sesquioxide) are loose in the soil forming the side of a ravine marking the northwest end of the limestone exposure.

Bear Basin.—Miners and prospectors working on the North Fork Snoqualmie River report that large clear quartz crystals occur rather plentifully in a rock slide near the Bear Basin prospects. Further details are unknown but should be available from the miners.

Devil's Canyon.—In the S½ sec. 27, T. 25 N., R. 10 E., 300 feet above the Devil's Canyon prospect, is a vuggy zone about 400 feet wide in which are many clusters of clear quartz crystals. The individual crystals are mostly less than 2 inches long and ½ inch in diameter.

Clipper property.—In the north center of sec. 1, T. 23 N., R. 11 E., a vuggy zone contains clear quartz crystals.

KITTITAS COUNTY
AGATES

Virden locality.—Beautifully colored blue agates have been found in and near Horse Canyon, 1 to 2 miles south of Virden (also known as McCallum and Lauderdale Lodge), in the W½ sec. 34, T. 20 N., R. 17 E.

Liberty locality.—It is reported that rather abundant agate-filled geodes occur at the extreme heads of Williams Creek, Boulder Creek, and, particularly, an unnamed creek between these two. The head of the unnamed creek is about 5 miles northeast of Liberty at an altitude of 5,000 feet or so. All these streams head just below the precipitous escarpment forming the west side of Table Mountain. The mountain is capped by flows of Yakima basalt which are immediately underlain by flows and tuff beds of the Teanaway basalt. The latter is probably the source of the geodes; certainly it is favorable for their occurrence.

Chalcedony occurs as amygdules and as fillings in larger irregular cavities in the Teanaway basalt, which crops out in an east-west belt 2 miles wide that is crossed by the highway (U. S. 97) just south of Liberty. Specimens, including blue agates, have been found in road cuts and in the hills on either side of the highway.

Redtop-Cle Elum Lake locality.—The exposures of Teanaway basalt extend west of Liberty for about 5 miles, then swing to the north for about 8 miles, then extend westward some 17 miles to Cle Elum Lake. Throughout this distance the belt is from 1 to 4 miles in width. West of Cle Elum Lake the formation is exposed to a width of from ½ mile to 4 miles from near the junction of the Cle Elum and Yakima Rivers northwestward for at least 26 miles.[1] It would appear that the whole area of Teanaway basalt exposures is favorable for the occurrence of chalcedonic nodules and geodes. Attractive agates, some of a beautiful blue color, have been collected on Redtop, 5 miles northwest of Liberty; they have been reported on Crystal Mountain, in the vicinity of Ryepatch, which is 4½ miles west of Redtop; at Elbow Peak, in sec. 6, T. 21 N., R. 15 E., on a small island (during high water) near the west shore of Cle Elum Lake; and on Mount Baldy (Domerie Peak?) west of Cle Elum Lake.

Four exposures of rhyolite in the general Ryepatch vicinity should be investigated, as it is probable that agate nodules will be found there. These are: (1) an area of about three-fourths of a square mile, centering in the SE¼ sec. 1, T. 21 N., R. 15 E., and a connected area of about a square mile centering in the SW¼ sec. 11 of the same township; (2) an area of about three-fourths of a square mile centering in the southeast corner of sec. 7, T. 21 N., R. 16 E.; (3) an area of nearly a square mile centering in the SE¼ sec. 15, T. 21 N., R. 16 E.; and (4) a small area of possibly one-eighth of a square mile centering in the NE¼SW¼ sec. 24, T. 21 N., R. 16 E. It is possible that these are erosional remnants of a once much more extensive rhyolite flow and that some, at least, of the finds of agate nodules mentioned above represent material weathered from this original source.

Squaw Creek locality.—An old report of 1913 mentions onyx agate having been found as massive interbasalt-flow filling in the Squaw Creek area nearly on the Kittitas-Yakima County line about 10 miles east of the Yakima River. It is said that some was sold to a California lapidary as gem material.

Ellensburg locality.—Another old report mentions lavendar-blue chalcedony having been gathered in the sagebrush country around Ellensburg. No further location details are given.

OPALIZED WOOD

Ginkgo Petrified Forest State Park.—This is an area of 9½ square miles lying just west of the Columbia River and crossed by U. S. Highway 10. Two museums are maintained: one is about ½ mile and the other about 2½ miles from the bridge over the Columbia River at Vantage. An abundance of opalized wood, ranging from flakes to nearly whole logs, occurs in the park area. Small fragments may be found on the surface of the ground and in the soil. Larger pieces and logs are in place (where originally opalized), encased in basalt, lying between basalt flows, and in interbasalt pumiceous

[1] U. S. Geol. Survey Geol. Atlas, Mount Stuart and Snoqualmie folios (nos. 106 and 139), 1904, 1906.

sediments; many of the pieces have been naturally exposed by erosion or have been uncovered by dug pits. No collecting is permitted in the park, but opalized wood similar to that of the park occurs under similar conditions outside the park area in the eastern part of Kittitas County. Collecting should be good in the westerly extension of the Saddle Mountains, between Kittitas and West Beverly.

COMMON OPAL

A greenish-yellow brittle massive opal occurs as small to huge nodules, as irregular masses, and sometimes as veinlike bodies in the diatomite beds of the Kittitas region and in those of the Quincy region of Grant County. It probably represents a segregation and deposition of silica derived from the solution of some of the diatomite, which, incidentally, is itself a form of opal. The material is cellular and laminated in concentric layers, has an unattractive appearance, and is only collected as a curiosity.

KLICKITAT COUNTY
OPALIZED WOOD

Roosevelt locality.—An area of some 360 square miles in eastern Klickitat County is favorable for the occurrence of opalized wood, though the hills north of Roosevelt have received the most attention. The material is similar to that of Kittitas and Grant Counties and occurs under similar conditions. The draws and gullies between Rock Creek on the west and Alder Creek and its tributaries on the east dissect the lava flows, occasionally expose larger logs, and commonly carry smaller pieces and flakes that become a guide for prospecting.

LEWIS COUNTY
AGATES AND JASPER

Newaukum River locality.—A region greatly favored by collectors is the Newaukum River drainage of central Lewis County. Agates of considerable size and commonly of good color are found along that stream and its tributaries. In fact, conditions are relatively good for the occurrence of agates all along the front of basalt hills, extending from north to south across the country and forming the more westerly outliers of the Cascade Range. Chalcedonic nodules, together with considerable jasper, have formed here in cavities in the basalt. They have weathered out as the basalt decomposed, or have been eroded out by frost and stream action, and then have been carried westward and deposited in the stream gravels, on the bedrock, and in the Pleistocene alluvium, sometimes far from their place of formation. Collecting is not as good as formerly but is still fair, particularly after high water has brought in new material or has reworked older gravels and uncovered specimens that had been buried.

An interesting present source of agates and jasper is the Pleistocene bedrock cover. In some places this sand and clay mantle is very thick; in others, only a thin veneer. The farther from the basalt exposures of the Cascade foothills or elsewhere, the more opportunity there has been for ordinary rock fragments to be eliminated (through comminution to sand or decomposition to clay) and, hence, for the harder, tougher agate nodules to be isolated. They may be found where the soil has been washed away, leaving them exposed on the surface of the ground; or in the beds of streams that are flowing through and reworking the alluvium mantle; or in road cuts where the Pleistocene deposits have been excavated.

Chehalis River locality.—Hundreds of pounds of agates have been taken from the cuts and roadside ditches of State Highway 12, between Adna and Pe Ell. When the road cuts in secs. 24 and 25, T. 13 N., R. 4 W. were fresh, collecting was remarkably good, as nearly every pebble remaining in the sandy clay of the banks or washed down into the drainage ditch was an agate. Any new road in this vicinity is almost invariably productive of material of interest to the collector.

Centralia vicinity.—An abundance of agate flakes and fragments occurs on the ground surface of the west part of the Towner farm, 4½ miles east of Centralia, in the S½NE¼ sec. 12, T. 14 N., R. 2 W. This material, although worthless in itself because of small size, indicates that a careful search of the vicinity is warranted in the expectation of finding larger agates of attractive color.

PLASMA

An opaque, rather dull green chert, sometimes described as plasma, occurs as cavity fillings and irregular vein-like masses a few inches in width in the basalt of an abandoned road-rock quarry on a ridge south of the Skookumchuck River; this is near the head of Fall Creek, in the NW¼NW¼ sec. 35, T. 15 N., R. 1 E. A similar material, but containing specks of jasper and so described as bloodstone, occurs as loose boulders in the soil of a hillside immediately east of the quarry. Material worth collecting is not abundant but may be found by diligent searching throughout most of the region where basalt forms the bedrock.

PETRIFIED WOOD

Petrified wood is a common accompaniment of the coal of southwestern Washington. It is silicified but not opalized and, although showing original grain to good advantage, is usually dark gray to black and unattractive in appearance. Occasional specimens are nearly white in outer parts (possibly from bleaching or removal of carbon) and so present an interesting contrast with the black interior when cut and polished.

PERIDOT

Doty locality.—A bed composed entirely of loosely consolidated crystals of olivine, an iron-magnesium silicate, occurs interbedded with Eocene tuff near the center of sec. 15, T. 14 N., R. 5 W. Although the crystals are small, some are of gem quality and so should be classed as peridot, the clear green variety of olivine.

LINCOLN COUNTY

PRECIOUS OPAL

Davenport locality.—An old report mentions the discovery of fire opals near Davenport but gives no details. Fernquist,[1] in commenting on this, stated that he had found precious opal in vesicular basalt at two places in this vicinity: one, on the Kurtz farm, one-half mile north of Mondovi; and a second, a mile northwest of Mondovi.

MASON COUNTY

(See Clallam and Grays Harbor Counties.)

OKANOGAN COUNTY

THULITE

Tunk Creek.—Thulite, the pink variety of zoisite, a calcium aluminum silicate, occurs in lenses 3 feet across in a hornblende schist near Tunk Creek, in the N½ sec. 5, T. 35 N., R. 27 E. Some has been mined and used for brooches and as an ornamental facing stone.

TURQUOISE

Nespelem district.—A single specimen of turquoise was brought to the Division of Geology in 1937 for identification. It was found at a mining prospect on the Twin Pine, Eureka, or Sunflower claim, near the north center sec. 4, T. 31 N., R. 30 E.

QUARTZ CRYSTAL

Early Winters Creek.—A "deposit" of large slightly smoky quartz crystals is said to occur on the mountain just northwest of the lower part of the creek. No other details are available.

Toroda Creek.—Prospectors from the area adjacent to the headwaters of the East Fork Toroda Creek have reported that rather large quartz crystals have been found in their workings.

PACIFIC COUNTY

AGATES

Bear River locality.—Agates have been found among gravel concentrations on bedrock at the base of Pleistocene sands and clays in the NW¼ sec. 5, T. 10 N., R. 10 E. This is in a highway cut 2 miles north of the mouth of Bear River, but agates should be expected under similar conditions at many other places in the county.

---

[1] Fernquist, C. O., Personal communication.

CHALCEDONIC FOSSIL CASTS

Willapa locality.—Light-gray and yellowish-gray chalcedony casts of fossil pelecypods (clams), having no trace of shell remaining, have been found in considerable numbers in the vicinity of Willapa. Some specimens are in excellent condition, and a great many contain entrapped water, sometimes with a bubble that moves as the fossil is revolved. These are similar to water-bearing chalcedony nodules termed "enhydros." The most productive collecting method has been to wade at low water in the muddy stream, particularly near and in the mouths of tributary creeks, and examine all pebbles felt by the bare feet.

PEND OREILLE COUNTY

AMETHYST

Newport locality.—Amethystine quartz has been found with white and clear quartz in the vein of the Ries Mining Co. on the west bank of the Pend Oreille River 2 miles north of Newport, in sec. 12, T. 31 N., R. 45 E.[1]

THULITE

Timber Mountain.—Crystals of thulite have been found at three places on and near Timber Mountain, which is near the center of sec. 29, T. 36 N., R. 43 E.: (1) near the peak of the mountain, (2) in the west center sec. 29, and (3) in the south center sec. 32.[2] The crystals were all small (some as much as one-fourth of an inch long, mostly smaller), so are probably without value, but they indicate the possibilities of, particularly, pegmatite dikes of the area.

PIERCE COUNTY

AMETHYSTINE QUARTZ

Old Siegmund ranch.—A mile east of Clay City, near the center of the W½ sec. 30, T. 17 N., R. 5 E. A 25-foot quartz vein was shown to be somewhat amethystine when it was explored for gold by means of a tunnel driven many years ago. Some amethystine quartz is exposed in detached masses or small isolated outcrops along the strike of the vein in the hillside above the tunnel, and a slightly amethystine 2-foot quartz vein, that may be a continuation of the main vein or an offshoot from it, crops out at an elevation of about 1,400 feet near the hilltop beyond the bench lying east of the main vein.

SAN JUAN COUNTY

It is reported that fossil brachiopod and nautilus shells, replaced by white and brown chalcedony, were displayed at an exposition

---

[1] Jenkins, O. P., Lead deposits of Pend Oreille and Stevens Counties: Washington Div. Geology Bull. 31, p. 46, 1924.

[2] Park, C. F., Jr., and Cannon, R. S., Jr., Geology and ore deposits of the Metaline quadrangle, Washington: U. S. Geol. Survey Prof. Paper 202, p. 57, 1943.

held in Seattle and that a considerable number were sold. They were obtained in the San Juan Islands (at Sucia Island?).[1]

SKAGIT COUNTY
"NEPHRITE JADE"

Sedro Woolley locality.—A hard dark-green magnesium silicate rock occurs as lenses or nodules in serpentine about 5 miles southeast of Sedro Woolley, in the NW¼NW¼ sec. 16, T. 34 N., R. 5 E. The material has somewhat puzzling optical properties, so that on the basis of petrographic study it has been variously classified as nephrite jade, silicified serpentine, and anthophyllite. The occurrence was formerly controlled by Mr. James Stephens (now deceased), who sold some as jade. Later it became part of the property (quarry?) of the Northwest Talc & Magnesium Co., so may have been mined out.

A similar material, also reported to be nephrite jade, is said to occur adjacent to a body of amphibole asbestos in serpentine on the Scott claim, in the SW¼SE¼ sec. 27, T. 36 N., R. 5 E., about 6 miles northeast of Sedro Woolley.

SKAMANIA COUNTY
CHALCEDONY

Stevenson locality.—Buff-gray chalcedony has been found near the east fork of Spring Creek, about 4 miles northwest of Stevenson. Some of the material represented nearly the entire fillings of collapsed cavities and was as much as 10 inches in length. All occurred in the surface soil, though doubtless originating in the basalt of the region.

AMETHYST

Rainbow prospect.—A small amount of amethystine quartz shows on the dump of a shaft on the Rainbow prospect, 2½ miles northeast of Washougal, in the NW¼ sec. 5, T. 2 N., R. 5 E.

OPAL

Wind River locality.—The lava buttes on Wind River, about 17 miles, airline, north of Carson, are said to contain opals as amygdules. The variety and exact location are not known.

SNOHOMISH COUNTY
GARNET

Vesper Peak locality.—The 48-55 prospect is near the center of sec. 9, T. 29 N., R. 10 E. at an altitude of 5,500 feet on the northeast rim of Sultan Basin. It is held as a mineral claim by Mr. P. C. Crane of Snohomish. Garnet, probably of the variety grossularite, occurs

---

[1]Sterrett, D. B., Gems and precious stones: U. S. Geol. Survey Mineral Resources, 1909, p. 740, 1911.

both massively and as spectacular clusters of intergrown crystals lining cavities. A small amount of chalcedony is present, and various other minerals are found in association with the garnet.[1]

QUARTZ CRYSTALS

Silvertip Peak.—A few clear quartz crystals have been found near the Weden Creek-Silver Creek divide, to the southeast of the Mackinaw prospect. One of these crystals is said to have been 4 inches long and 2 inches in diameter; a clump of crystals, somewhat iron-stained, was 5 inches across and included some 30 individuals ranging from a fraction of an inch to 3 inches in length.

STEVENS COUNTY

Colville locality.—A small vein of thulite, about half an inch thick, occurs at the Smoky Bullion property, in the NE¼ sec. 3, T. 37 N., R. 39 E.

THURSTON COUNTY
AGATES, JASPER, AND PETRIFIED WOOD

As in Cowlitz and Lewis Counties, agates and related collector's items occur in the area of basalt of the eastern part of Thurston County and may be found under conditions and in places similar to those described in some detail under the heading of Lewis County. Collections have been made in the vicinity of Tono by finding places where the surface mantle of Pleistocene sedimentary material is thin, digging through it to bedrock, and then examining the pebbles and larger rock fragments that form a sparse accumulation on the bedrock surface. Interesting chalcedonic material, including a minutely banded opaque green chert, has been found in the canyon of the Skookumchuck River, south of Vail.

WHITMAN COUNTY
PRECIOUS OPAL

Whelan locality.—This occurrence is on the Odonnell farm, on the west line of the SW¼ sec. 20, T. 15 N., R. 46 E., about 3 miles east of Whelan Grange and about 7 miles northeast of Pullman. Precious opal, occurring as amygdules in basalt, was discovered here in the bottom 4 feet of a 22-foot well dug in 1890 on what was then the William Leasure farm. In 1891-2 several pits were opened and gem stones to the value of nearly $6,000 were mined and sold. Kunz[2] reports that "the opal is fine, in many respects equal to the best material from Hungarian or Australian mines." He mentions that the gems vary from the size of a half pea to that of a hen's egg, the smaller ones being very rich in color but the larger ones often having

---

[1]Carithers, Ward, and Guard, A. K., Geology and ore deposits of the Sultan Basin, Snohomish County, Washington: Washington Div. Mines and Geology Bull. 36, p. 70, 1945.

[2]Kunz, G. F., Precious stones: U. S. Geol. Survey Mineral Resources for 1891, pp. 549-550, 1893; and for 1892, p. 776, 1893.

little or no play in color. The work was carried on in open pits or quarries. As the largest opening progressed northward into a hill, the topsoil became deeper but the layer of basalt next to it and overlying the 4-foot opal-bearing stratum remained of about the same thickness. The opals occurred in "frozen" contact with the basalt matrix, as kernels in vesicles larger than the amygdule, and as loose stones in some places where the formerly surrounding basalt had decomposed to a "fat" very tenacious clay.

At the present time there is little to see in the old, grass-covered rubble piles, though occasionally milk opal and hyalite can be found, and there is always the possibility of finding precious opal in freshly broken basalt blocks. It is questionable, however, how much of the visible fragmental basalt is from the opal-bearing zone. As the land has a known value for wheat farming, it is doubtful that its prospective value for opal mining will be further tested.

Moses locality.—This is on the Snake River, 8 miles or so down river from Clarkston. Precious opal of excellent quality is reported[1] to have been found in a prospect hole high on the hillside. A visit to this place failed to verify the report, but common milk opal was found in scattered specimens. As some precious opal has been found in float along the railway below the prospect, it is reasonable to expect that further search in the vicinity of the prospect would be warranted.

SMOKY QUARTZ

Bald Butte.—At one time a considerable number of smoky-quartz crystals were found near Colton in a sand pit on the side of Bald Butte. Samples were brought by a Mr. Thomas to St. Scholasticas Academy, Colton, and there identified. Similar crystals have been found in the soil of the south slope of the Butte.

AMETHYSTINE QUARTZ

Ringo Hills.—It is reported that the hill west of Ringo Station, in sec. 18, T. 16 N., R. 46 E., and the nearest ridge to the northeast contain 75-foot bands of what appears to be vein quartz, traversing the usual quartzite of the hills; on the slope east of the railway some of this quartz is amethystine.[2]

YAKIMA COUNTY
AGATE

Zillah-Sunnyside locality.—It is reported that agates are abundant throughout a considerable area of old stream-worn gravels lying on a bench north of the Yakima River, in T. 10 N., R. 21 E. They have also been found in the present-day gravels of the river.

---

[1]The Mineralogist: vol. 7, no. 2, 1939.

[2]Hodge, E. T., Market for Columbia River hydroelectric power using Northwest minerals, Section 2, Northwest silica materials: U. S. Army Corps of Engineers, Portland, Oregon, vol. 1, pt. 1, pp. 75-76, 1938.

Naches locality.—In 1891 specimens of alternately layered black and brown chalcedony (onyx) were found in the Naches vicinity by Mr. E. K. Curr. The material was said to have been very beautiful after polishing.

JASPER

In the NE¼ sec. 12, T. 13 N., R. 18 E., close to or just west of the confluence of the Yakima and Naches Rivers, a 1-foot bed of red and maroon jasper and irregular yellow opal phases occurs between two basalt flows on the hillside above the river. Fragments of the material show as float below the outcrop.

OPALIZED WOOD

Barrel Springs locality.—Opalized wood is plentiful near the Sunnyside road a few miles south of its junction with the Yakima-Cold Springs road. Indians formerly had a chipping ground at Barrel Springs, half a mile or so south of the junction, where material for arrowheads was roughed out. Flakes of opalized wood in the dry gullies of the vicinity indicate the occurrence of larger masses up the gullies. One draw, crossed by the Sunnyside road about 4 miles south of the junction, has a spectacular amount of silicified and opalized wood; this is probably in sec. 35, T. 12 N., R. 23 E. Up the draw (south), a quarter of a mile or so from the road, a bed as much as 15 feet thick of a unique conglomerate crops out between basalt flows. The bed is almost entirely silicified and opalized wood, occurring as small and large fragments and even as whole sections of logs and stumps. The largest seen was 5 or 6 feet in diameter. Petrified branch sections and knots are interesting, but the general gray color of most of the "wood" is not attractive. Presumably the interior of the large pieces has a more pleasing color, as is usual in the eastern Washington occurrences.

OBSIDIAN

Obsidian, volcanic glass, is not common in Washington as it is in Oregon, and hardly any known in place has an appearance which would be of interest to collectors. However, water-worn obsidian pebbles—brilliantly black when broken—have been found on bars of the Yakima River above Prosser, and it is reported that massive obsidian as well as water-worn pebbles occur a mile or so south of the highway between Mabton and Bickleton.

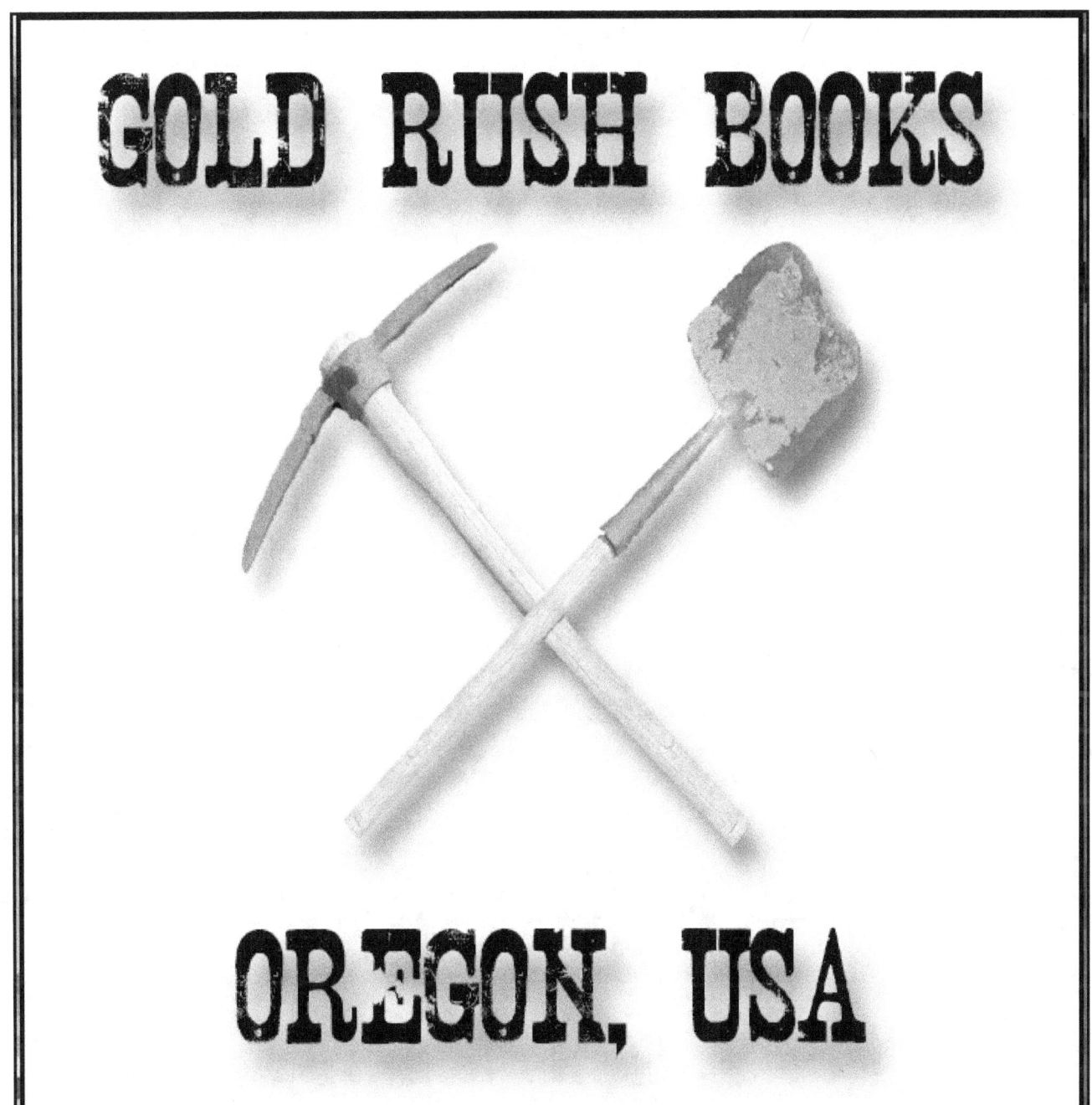

GOLD RUSH BOOKS

OREGON, USA

www.GoldMiningBooks.com

Books On Mining

Visit: www.goldminingbooks.com to order your copies or ask your favorite book seller to offer them.

Mining Books by Kerby Jackson

Gold Dust: Stories From Oregon's Mining Years - Oregon mining historian and prospector, Kerby Jackson, brings you a treasure trove of seventeen stories on Southern Oregon's rich history of gold prospecting, the prospectors and their discoveries, and the breathtaking areas they settled in and made homes. 5" X 8", 98 ppgs. Retail Price: $11.99

The Golden Trail: More Stories From Oregon's Mining Years - In his follow-up to "Gold Dust: Stories of Oregon's Mining Years", this time around, Jackson brings us twelve tales from Oregon's Gold Rush, including the story about the first gold strike on Canyon Creek in Grant County, about the old timers who found gold by the pail full at the Victor Mine near Galice, how Iradel Bray discovered a rich ledge of gold on the Coquille River during the height of the Rogue River War, a tale of two elderly miners on the hunt for a lost mine in the Cascade Mountains, details about the discovery of the famous Armstrong Nugget and others. 5" X 8", 70 ppgs. Retail Price: $10.99

Oregon Mining Books

Geology and Mineral Resources of Josephine County, Oregon - Unavailable since the 1970's, this important publication was originally compiled by the Oregon Department of Geology and Mineral Industries and includes important details on the economic geology and mineral resources of this important mining area in South Western Oregon. Included are notes on the history, geology and development of important mines, as well as insights into the mining of gold, copper, nickel, limestone, chromium and other minerals found in large quantities in Josephine County, Oregon. 8.5" X 11", 54 ppgs. Retail Price: $9.99

Mines and Prospects of the Mount Reuben Mining District - Unavailable since 1947, this important publication was originally compiled by geologist Elton Youngberg of the Oregon Department of Geology and Mineral Industries and includes detailed descriptions, histories and the geology of the Mount Reuben Mining District in Josephine County, Oregon. Included are notes on the history, geology, development and assay statistics, as well as underground maps of all the major mines and prospects in the vicinity of this much neglected mining district. 8.5" X 11", 48 ppgs. Retail Price: $9.99

The Granite Mining District - Notes on the history, geology and development of important mines in the well known Granite Mining District which is located in Grant County, Oregon. Some of the mines discussed include the Ajax, Blue Ribbon, Buffalo, Continental, Cougar-Independence, Magnolia, New York, Standard and the Tillicum. Also included are many rare maps pertaining to the mines in the area. 8.5" X 11", 48 ppgs. Retail Price: $9.99

Ore Deposits of the Takilma and Waldo Mining Districts of Josephine County, Oregon - The Waldo and Takilma mining districts are most notable for the fact that the earliest large scale mining of placer gold and copper in Oregon took place in these two areas. Included are details about some of the earliest large gold mines in the state such as the Llano de Oro, High Gravel, Cameron, Platerica, Deep Gravel and others, as well as copper mines such as the famous Queen of Bronze mine, the Waldo, Lily and Cowboy mines. This volume also includes six maps and 20 original illustrations. 8.5" X 11", 74 ppgs. Retail Price: $9.99

Metal Mines of Douglas, Coos and Curry Counties, Oregon - Oregon mining historian Kerby Jackson introduces us to a classic work on Oregon's mining history in this important re-issue of Bulletin 14C Volume 1, otherwise known as the Douglas, Coos & Curry Counties, Oregon Metal Mines Handbook. Unavailable since 1940, this important publication was originally compiled by the Oregon Department of Geology and Mineral Industries and includes detailed descriptions, histories and the geology of over 250 metallic mineral mines and prospects in this rugged area of South West Oregon. 8.5" X 11", 158 ppgs. Retail Price: $19.99

Metal Mines of Jackson County, Oregon - Unavailable since 1943, this important publication was originally compiled by the Oregon Department of Geology and Mineral Industries includes detailed descriptions, histories and the geology of over 450 metallic mineral mines and prospects in Jackson County, Oregon. Included are such famous gold mining areas as Gold Hill, Jacksonville, Sterling and the Upper Applegate. 8.5" X 11", 220 ppgs. Retail Price: $24.99

Metal Mines of Josephine County, Oregon - Oregon mining historian Kerby Jackson introduces us to a classic work on Oregon's mining history in this important re-issue of Bulletin 14C, otherwise known as the Josephine County, Oregon Metal Mines Handbook. Unavailable since 1952, this important publication was originally compiled by the Oregon Department of Geology and Mineral Industries includes detailed descriptions, histories and the geology of over 500 metallic mineral mines and prospects in Josephine County, Oregon. 8.5" X 11", 250 ppgs. Retail Price: $24.99

Metal Mines of North East Oregon - Oregon mining historian Kerby Jackson introduces us to a classic work on Oregon's mining history in this important re-issue of Bulletin 14A and 14B, otherwise known as the North East Oregon Metal Mines Handbook. Unavailable since 1941, this important publication was originally compiled by the Oregon Department of Geology and Mineral Industries and includes detailed descriptions, histories and the geology of over 750 metallic mineral mines and prospects in North Eastern Oregon. 8.5" X 11", 310 ppgs. Retail Price: $29.99

Metal Mines of North West Oregon - Oregon mining historian Kerby Jackson introduces us to a classic work on Oregon's mining history in this important re-issue of Bulletin 14D, otherwise known as the North West Oregon Metal Mines Handbook. Unavailable since 1951, this important publication was originally compiled by the Oregon Department of Geology and Mineral Industries and includes detailed descriptions, histories and the geology of over 250 metallic mineral mines and prospects in North Western Oregon. 8.5" X 11", 182 ppgs. Retail Price: $19.99

Mines and Prospects of Oregon - Mining historian Kerby Jackson introduces us to a classic mining work by the Oregon Bureau of Mines in this important re-issue of The Handbook of Mines and Prospects of Oregon. Unavailable since 1916, this publication includes important insights into hundreds of gold, silver, copper, coal, limestone and other mines that operated in the State of Oregon around the turn of the 19th Century. Included are not only geological details on early mines throughout Oregon, but also insights into their history, production, locations and in some cases, also included are rare maps of their underground workings. 8.5" X 11", 314 ppgs. Retail Price: $24.99

Lode Gold of the Klamath Mountains of Northern California and South West Oregon
(See California Mining Books)

Mineral Resources of South West Oregon - Unavailable since 1914, this publication includes important insights into dozens of mines that once operated in South West Oregon, including the famous gold fields of Josephine and Jackson Counties, as well as the Coal Mines of Coos County. Included are not only geological details on early mines throughout South West Oregon, but also insights into their history, production and locations. 8.5" X 11", 154 ppgs. Retail Price: $11.99

Chromite Mining in The Klamath Mountains of California and Oregon
(See California Mining Books)

Southern Oregon Mineral Wealth - Unavailable since 1904, this rare publication provides a unique snapshot into the mines that were operating in the area at the time. Included are not only geological details on early mines throughout South West Oregon, but also insights into their history, production and locations. Some of the mining areas include Grave Creek, Greenback, Wolf Creek, Jump Off Joe Creek, Granite Hill, Galice, Mount Reuben, Gold Hill, Galls Creek, Kane Creek, Sardine Creek, Birdseye Creek, Evans Creek, Foots Creek, Jacksonville, Ashland, the Applegate River, Waldo, Kerby and the Illinois River, Althouse and Sucker Creek, as well as insights into local copper mining and other topics. 8.5" X 11", 64 ppgs. Retail Price: $8.99

Geology and Ore Deposits of the Takilma and Waldo Mining Districts - Unavailable since the 1933, this publication was originally compiled by the United States Geological Survey and includes details on gold and copper mining in the Takilma and Waldo Districts of Josephine County, Oregon. The Waldo and Takilma mining districts are most notable for the fact that the earliest large scale mining of placer gold and copper in Oregon took place in these two areas. Included in this report are details about some of the earliest large gold mines in the state such as the Llano de Oro, High Gravel, Cameron, Platerica, Deep Gravel and others, as well as copper mines such as the famous Queen of Bronze mine, the Waldo, Lily and Cowboy mines. In addition to geological examinations, insights are also provided into the production, day to day operations and early histories of these mines, as well as calculations of known mineral reserves in the area. This volume also includes six maps and 20 original illustrations. 8.5" X 11", 74 ppgs. Retail Price: $9.99

Gold Mines of Oregon - Oregon mining historian Kerby Jackson introduces us to a classic work on Oregon's mining history in this important re-issue of Bulletin 61, otherwise known as "Gold and Silver In Oregon". Unavailable since 1968, this important publication was originally compiled by geologists Howard C. Brooks and Len Ramp of the Oregon Department of Geology and Mineral Industries and includes detailed descriptions, histories and the geology of over 450 gold mines Oregon. Included are notes on the history, geology and gold production statistics of all the major mining areas in Oregon including the Klamath Mountains, the Blue Mountains and the North Cascades. While gold is where you find it, as every miner knows, the path to success is to prospect for gold where it was previously found. **8.5" X 11", 344 ppgs. Retail Price: $24.99**

Mines and Mineral Resources of Curry County Oregon - Originally published in 1916, this important publication on Oregon Mining has not been available for nearly a century. Included are rare insights into the history, production and locations of dozens of gold mines in Curry County, Oregon, as well as detailed information on important Oregon mining districts in that area such as those at Agness, Bald Face Creek, Mule Creek, Boulder Creek, China Diggings, Collier Creek, Elk River, Gold Beach, Rock Creek, Sixes River and elsewhere. Particular attention is especially paid to the famous beach gold deposits of this portion of the Oregon Coast. **8.5" X 11", 140 ppgs. Retail Price: $11.99**

Chromite Mining in South West Oregon - Originally published in 1961, this important publication on Oregon Mining has not been available for nearly a century. Included are rare insights into the history, production and locations of nearly 300 chromite mines in South Western Oregon. **8.5" X 11", 184 ppgs. Retail Price: $14.99**

Mineral Resources of Douglas County Oregon - Originally published in 1972, this important publication on Oregon Mining has not been available for nearly forty years. Included are rare insights into the geology, history, production and locations of numerous gold mines and other mining properties in Douglas County, Oregon. **8.5" X 11", 124 ppgs. Retail Price: $11.99**

Mineral Resources of Coos County Oregon - Originally published in 1972, this important publication on Oregon Mining has not been available for nearly forty years. Included are rare insights into the geology, history, production and locations of numerous gold mines and other mining properties in Coos County, Oregon. **8.5" X 11", 100 ppgs. Retail Price: $11.99**

Mineral Resources of Lane County Oregon - Originally published in 1938, this important publication on Oregon Mining has not been available for nearly seventy five years. Included are extremely rare insights into the geology and mines of Lane County, Oregon, in particular in the Bohemia, Blue River, Oakridge, Black Butte and Winberry Mining Districts. **8.5" X 11", 82 ppgs. Retail Price: $9.99**

Mineral Resources of the Upper Chetco River of Oregon: Including the Kalmiopsis Wilderness - Originally published in 1975, this important publication on Oregon Mining has not been available for nearly forty years. Withdrawn under the 1872 Mining Act since 1984, real insight into the minerals resources and mines of the Upper Chetco River has long been unavailable due to the remoteness of the area. Despite this, the decades of battle between property owners and environmental extremists over the last private mining inholding in the area has continued to pique the interest of those interested in mining and other forms of natural resource use. Gold mining began in the area in the 1850's and has a rich history in this geographic area, even if the facts surrounding it are little known. Included are twenty two rare photographs, as well as insights into the Becca and Morning Mine, the Emmly Mine (also known as Emily Camp), the Frazier Mine, the Golden Dream or Higgins Mine, Hustis Mine, Peck Mine and others. **8.5" X 11", 64 ppgs. Retail Price: $8.99**

Gold Dredging in Oregon - Originally published in 1939, this important publication on Oregon Mining has not been available for nearly seventy five years. Included are extremely rare insights into the history and day to day operations of the dragline and bucketline gold dredges that once worked the placer gold fields of South West and North East Oregon in decades gone by. Also included are details into the areas that were worked by gold dredges in Josephine, Jackson, Baker and Grant counties, as well as the economic factors that impacted this mining method. This volume also offers a unique look into the values of river bottom land in relation to both farming and mining, in how farm lands were mined, re-soiled and reclamated after the dredges worked them. Featured are hard to find maps of the gold dredge fields, as well as rare photographs from a bygone era. **8.5" X 11", 86 ppgs. Retail Price: $8.99**

Quick Silver Mining in Oregon - Originally published in 1963, this important publication on Oregon Mining has not been available for over fifty years. This publication includes details into the history and production of Elemental Mercury or Quicksilver in the State of Oregon. **8.5" X 11", 238 ppgs. Retail Price: $15.99**

Mines of the Greenhorn Mining District of Grant County Oregon - Originally published in 1948, this important publication on Oregon Mining has not been available for over sixty five years. In this publication are rare insights into the mines of the famous Greenhorn Mining District of Grant County, Oregon, especially the famous Morning Mine. Also included are details on the Tempest, Tiger, Bi-Metallic, Windsor, Psyche, Big Johnny, Snow Creek, Banzette and Paramount Mines, as well as prospects in the vicinities in the famous mining areas of Mormon Basin, Vinegar Basin and Desolation Creek. Included are hard to find mine maps and dozens of rare photographs from the bygone era of Grant County's rich mining history. **8.5" X 11", 72 ppgs. Retail Price: $9.99**

Geology of the Wallowa Mountains of Oregon: Part I (Volume 1) - Originally published in 1938, this important publication on Oregon Mining has not been available for nearly seventy five years. Included are details on the geology of this unique portion of North Eastern Oregon. This is the first part of a two book series on the area. Accompanying the text are rare photographs and historic maps.**8.5" X 11"**, **92 ppgs. Retail Price: $9.99**

Geology of the Wallowa Mountains of Oregon: Part II (Volume 2) - Originally published in 1938, this important publication on Oregon Mining has not been available for nearly seventy five years. Included are details on the geology of this unique portion of North Eastern Oregon. This is the first part of a two book series on the area. Accompanying the text are rare photographs and historic maps.**8.5" X 11"**, **94 ppgs. Retail Price: $9.99**

Field Identification of Minerals For Oregon Prospectors - Originally published in 1940, this important publication on Oregon Mining has not been available for nearly seventy five years. Included in this volume is an easy system for testing and identifying a wide range of minerals that might be found by prospectors, geologists and rockhounds in the State of Oregon, as well as in other locales. Topics include how to put together your own field testing kit and how to conduct rudimentary tests in the field. This volume is written in a clear and concise way to make it useful even for beginners. **8.5" X 11"**, **158 ppgs. Retail Price: $14.99**

The Bohemia Mining District of Oregon - Originally published in 1900, this important publication on Oregon Mining has not been available for over a century. Included in this volume are important insights into the famous Bohemia Mining District of Oregon, including the histories and locations of important gold mines in the area such as the Ophir Mine, Clarence, Acturas, Peek-a-boo, White Swan, Combination Mine, the Musick Mine, The California, White Ghost, The Mystery, Wall Street, Vesuvius, Story, Lizzie Bullock, Delta, Elsie Dora, Golden Slipper, Broadway, Champion Mine, Knott, Noonday, Helena, White Wings, Riverside and others. Also included are notes on the nearby Blue River Mining District. **8.5" X 11"**, **58 ppgs. Retail Price: $9.99**

The Gold Fields of Eastern Oregon - Unavailable since 1900, this publication was originally compiled by the Baker City Chamber of Commerce Offering important insights into the gold mining history of Eastern Oregon, "The Gold Fields of Eastern Oregon" sheds a rare light on many of the gold mines that were operating at the turn of the 19th Century in Baker County and Grant County in North Eastern Oregon. Some of the areas featured include the Cable Cove District, Baisely-Elhorn, Granite, Red Boy, Bonanza, Susanville, Sparta, Virtue, Vaughn, Sumpter, Burnt River, Rye Valley and other mining districts. Included is basic information on not only many gold mines that are well known to those interested in Eastern Oregon mining history, but also many mines and prospects which have been mostly lost to the passage of time. Accompanying are numerous rare photos **8.5" X 11"**, **78 ppgs. Retail Price: $10.99**

Gold Mining in Eastern Oregon - Originally published in 1938, this important publication on Oregon Mining has not been available for over a century. Included in this volume are important insights into the famous mining districts of Eastern Oregon during the late 1930's. Particular attention is given to those gold mines with milling and concentrating facilities in the Greenhorn, Red Boy, Alamo, Bonanza, Granite, Cable Cove, Cracker Creek, Virtue, Keating, Medical Springs, Sanger, Sparta, Chicken Creek, Mormon Basin, Connor Creek, Cornucopia and the Bull Run Mining Districts. Some of the mines featured include the Ben Harrison, North Pole-Columbia, Highland Maxwell, Baisley-Elkhorn, White Swan, Balm Creek, Twin Baby, Gem of Sparta, New Deal, Gleason, Gifford-Johnson, Cornucopia, Record, Bull Run, Orion and others. Of particular interest are the mill flow sheets and descriptions of milling operations of these mines. **8.5" X 11"**, **68 ppgs. Retail Price: $8.99**

The Gold Belt of the Blue Mountains of Oregon - Originally published in 1901, this important publication on Oregon Mining has not been available for over a century. Included in this volume are rare insights into the gold deposits of the Blue Mountains of North East Oregon, including the history of their early discovery and early production. Extensive details are offered on this important mining area's mineralogy and economic geology, as well as insights into nearby gold placers, silver deposits and copper deposits. Featured are the Elkhorn and Rock Creek mining districts, the Pocahontas district, Auburn and Minersville districts, Sumpter and Cracker Creek, Cable Cove, the Camp Carson district, Granite, Alamo, Greenhorn, Robinsonville, the Upper Burnt River Valley and Bonanza districts, Susanville, Quartzburg, Canyon Creek, Virtue, the Copper Butte district, the North Powder River, Sparta, Eagle Creek, Cornucopia, Pine Creek, Lower Powder River, the Upper Snake River Canyon, Rye Valley, Lower Burnt River Valley, Mormon Basin, the Malheur and Clarks Creek districts, Sutton Creek and others. Of particular interest are important details on numerous gold mines and prospects in these mining districts, including their locations, histories, geology and other important information, as well as information on silver, copper and fire opal deposits. **8.5" X 11"**, **250 ppgs. Retail Price: $24.99**

<u>Mining in the Cascades Range of Oregon</u> - Originally published in 1938, this important publication on Oregon Mining has not been available for over seventy five years. Included in this volume are rare insights into the gold mines and other types of metal mines in the Cascades Mountain Range of Oregon. Some of the important mining areas covered include the famous Bohemia Mining District, the North Santiam Mining District, Quartzville Mining District, Blue River Mining District, Fall Creek Mining District, Oakridge District, Zinc District, Buzzard-Al Sarena District, Grand Cove, Climax District and Barron Mining District. Of particular interest are important details on over 100 mines and prospects in these mining districts, including their locations, histories, geology and other important information. **8.5" X 11", 170 ppgs. Retail Price: $14.99**

<u>Beach Gold Placers of the Oregon Coast</u> - Originally published in 1934, this important publication on Oregon Mining has not been available for over 80 years. Included in this volume are rare insights into the beach gold deposits of the State of Oregon, including their locations, occurance, composition and geology. Of particular interest is information on placer platinum in Oregon's rich beach deposits. Also included are the locations and other information on some famous Oregon beach mines, including the Pioneer, Eagle, Chickamin, Iowa and beach placer mines north of the mouth of the Rogue River. **8.5" X 11", 60 ppgs. Retail Price: $8.99**

Idaho Mining Books

Gold in Idaho - Unavailable since the 1940's, this publication was originally compiled by the Idaho Bureau of Mines and includes details on gold mining in Idaho. Included is not only raw data on gold production in Idaho, but also valuable insight into where gold may be found in Idaho, as well as practical information on the gold bearing rocks and other geological features that will assist those looking for placer and lode gold in the State of Idaho. This volume also includes thirteen gold maps that greatly enhance the practical usability of the information contained in this small book detailing where to find gold in Idaho. **8.5" X 11", 72 ppgs. Retail Price: $9.99**

Geology of the Couer D'Alene Mining District of Idaho - Unavailable since 1961, this publication was originally compiled by the Idaho Bureau of Mines and Geology and includes details on the mining of gold, silver and other minerals in the famous Coeur D'Alene Mining District in Northern Idaho. Included are details on the early history of the Coeur D'Alene Mining District, local tectonic settings, ore deposit features, information on the mineral belts of the Osburn Fault, as well as detailed information on the famous Bunker Hill Mine, the Dayrock Mine, Galena Mine, Lucky Friday Mine and the infamous Sunshine Mine. This volume also includes sixteen hard to find maps. **8.5" X 11", 70 ppgs. Retail Price: $9.99**

The Gold Camps and Silver Cities of Idaho - Originally published in 1963, this important publication on Idaho Mining has not been available for nearly fifty years. Included are rare insights into the history of Idaho's Gold Rush, as well as the mad craze for silver in the Idaho Panhandle. Documented in fine detail are the early mining excitements at Boise Basin, at South Boise, in the Owyhees, at Deadwood, Long Valley, Stanley Basin and Robinson Bar, at Atlanta, on the famous Boise River, Volcano, Little Smokey, Banner, Boise Ridge, Hailey, Leesburg, Lemhi, Pearl, at South Mountain, Shoup and Ulysses, Yellow Jacket and Loon Creek. The story follows with the appearance of Chinese miners at the new mining camps on the Snake River, Black Pine, Yankee Fork, Bay Horse, Clayton, Heath, Seven Devils, Gibbonsville, Vienna and Sawtooth City. Also included are special sections on the Idaho Lead and Silver mines of the late 1800's, as well as the mining discoveries of the early 1900's that paved the way for Idaho's modern mining and mineral industry. Lavishly illustrated with rare historic photos, this volume provides a one of a kind documentary into Idaho's mining history that is sure to be enjoyed by not only modern miners and prospectors who still scour the hills in search of nature's treasures, but also those enjoy history and tromping through overgrown ghost towns and long abandoned mining camps. **8.5" X 11", 186 ppgs. Retail Price: $14.99**

Ore Deposits and Mining in North Western Custer County Idaho - Unavailable since 1913, this important publication was originally published by the Us Department of the Interior and has been unavailable for a century. Included are fine details on the geology, geography, gold placers and gold and silver bearing quartz veins of the mining region of North West Custer County, Idaho. Of particular interest is a rare look at the mines and prospects of the region, including those such as the Ramshorn Mine, SkyLark, Riverview, Excelsior, Beardsley, Pacific, Hoosier, Silver Brick, Forest Rose and dozens of others in the Bay Horse Mining District. Also covered are the mines of the Yankee Fork District such as the Lucky Boy, Badger, Black, Enterprise, Charles Dickens, Morrison, Golden Sunbeam, Montana, Golden Gate and others, as well as those in the Loon Mining District. **8.5" X 11", 126 ppgs. Retail Price: $12.99**

Gold Rush To Idaho - Unavailable since 1963, this important publication was originally published by the Idaho Bureau of Mines and has been unavailable for 50 years. "Gold Rush To Idaho" revisits the earliest years of the discovery of gold in Idaho Territory and introduces us to the conditions that the pioneer gold seekers met when they blazed a trail through the wilderness of Idaho's mountains and discovered the precious yellow metal at Oro Fino and Pierce. Subsequent rushes followed at places like Elk City, Newsome, Clearwater Station, Florence, Warrens and elsewhere. Of particular interest is a rare look at the hardships that the first miners in Idaho met with during their day to day existences and their attempts to bring law and order to their mining camps. **8.5" X 11", 88 ppgs. Retail Price: $9.99**

The Geology and Mines of Northern Idaho and North Western Montana - Unavailable since 1909, this important publication was originally published by the Us Department of the Interior and has been unavailable for a century. Included are fine details on the geology and geography of the mining regions of Northern Idaho and North Western Montana. Of particular interest is a rare look at the mines and prospects of the region, including those in the Pine Creek Mining District, Lake Pend Oreille district, Troy Mining District, Sylvanite District, Cabinet Mining District, Prospect Mining District and the Missoula Valley. Some of the mines featured include the Iron Mountain, Silver Butte, Snowshoe, Grouse Mountain Mine and others. **8.5" X 11", 142 ppgs. Retail Price: $12.99**

Mining in the Alturas Quadrangle of Blaine County Idaho - Unavailable since 1922, this important publication was originally published by the Idaho Bureau of Mines and has been unavailable for ninety years. Topics include the geology, rock formations and the formation of ore deposits in this important mining area of Idaho. Of particular focus is information on the local geology, quartz veins and ore deposits of this portion of Idaho. Included are hard to find details, including the descriptions and locations of numerous gold and silver mines in the area including the Silver King, Pilgrim, Columbia, Lone Jack, Sunbeam, Pride of the West, Lucky Boy, Scotia, Atlanta, Beaver-Bidwell and others mines and prospects. **8.5" X 11", 56 ppgs. Retail Price: $8.99**

Mining in Lemhi County Idaho - Originally published in 1913, this important book on Idaho Mining has not been available to miners for over a century. Included are rare insights into hundreds of gold, silver, copper and other mines in this famous Idaho mining area. Details include the locations, geology, history, production and other facts of the mines of this region, not only gold and silver hardrock mines, but also gold placer mines, lead-silver deposits, copper mines, cobalt-nickel deposits, tungsten and tin mines . It is lavishly illustrated with hard to find photos of the period and rare mining maps. Some of the vicinities featured include the Nicholia Mining District, Spring Mountain District, Texas District, Blue Wing District, Junction District, McDevitt District, Pratt Creek, Eldorado District, Kirtley Creek, Carmen Creek, Gibbonsville, Indian Creek, Mineral Hill District, Mackinaw, Eureka District, Blackbird District, YellowJacket District, Gravel Range District, Junction District, Parker Mountain and other mining districts. **8.5" X 11", 226 ppgs. Retail Price: $19.99**

Utah Mining Books

Fluorite in Utah - Unavailable since 1954, this publication was originally compiled by the USGS, State of Utah and U.S. Atomic Energy Commission and details the mining of fluorspar, also known as fluorite in the State of Utah. Included are details on the geology and history of fluorspar (fluorite) mining in Utah, including details on where this unique gem mineral may be found in the State of Utah. **8.5" X 11", 60 ppgs. Retail Price: $8.99**

California Mining Books

The Tertiary Gravels of the Sierra Nevada of California - Mining historian Kerby Jackson introduces us to a classic mining work by Waldemar Lindgren in this important re-issue of The Tertiary Gravels of the Sierra Nevada of California. Unavailable since 1911, this publication includes details on the gold bearing ancient river channels of the famous Sierra Nevada region of California. **8.5" X 11", 282 ppgs. Retail Price: $19.99**

The Mother Lode Mining Region of California - Unavailable since 1900, this publication includes details on the gold mines of California's famous Mother Lode gold mining area. Included are details on the geology, history and important gold mines of the region, as well as insights into historic mining methods, mine timbering, mining machinery, mining bell signals and other details on how these mines operated. Also included are insights into the gold mines of the California Mother Lode that were in operation during the first sixty years of California's mining history. **8.5" X 11", 176 ppgs. Retail Price: $14.99**

Lode Gold of the Klamath Mountains of Northern California and South West Oregon - Unavailable since 1971, this publication was originally compiled by Preston E. Hotz and includes details on the lode mining districts of Oregon and California's Klamath Mountains. Included are details on the geology, history and important lode mines of the French Gulch, Deadwood, Whiskeytown, Shasta, Redding, Muletown, South Fork, Old Diggings, Dog Creek (Delta), Bully Choop (Indian Creek), Harrison Gulch, Hayfork, Minersville, Trinity Center, Canyon Creek, East Fork, New River, Denny, Liberty (Black Bear), Cecilville, Callahan, Yreka, Fort Jones and Happy Camp mining districts in California, as well as the Ashland, Rogue River, Applegate, Illinois River, Takilma, Greenback, Galice, Silver Peak, Myrtle Creek and Mule Creek districts of South Western Oregon. Also included are insights into the mineralization and other characteristics of this important mining region. **8.5" X 11", 100 ppgs. Retail Price: $10.99**

Mines and Mineral Resources of Shasta County, Siskiyou County, Trinity County: California - Unavailable since 1915, this publication was originally compiled by the California State Mining Bureau and includes details on the gold mines of this area of Northern California. Also included are insights into the mineralization and other characteristics of this important mining region, as well as the location of historic gold mines. **8.5" X 11"**, 204 ppgs. **Retail Price: $19.99**

Geology of the Yreka Quadrangle, Siskiyou County, California - Unavailable since 1977, this publication was originally compiled by Preston E. Hotz and includes details on the geology of the Yreka Quadrangle of Siskiyou County, California. Also included are insights into the mineralization and other characteristics of this important mining region. **8.5" X 11"**, 78 ppgs. **Retail Price: $7.99**

Mines of San Diego and Imperial Counties, California - Originally published in 1914, this important publication on California Mining has not been available for a century. This publication includes important information on the early gold mines of San Diego and Imperial County, which were some of the first gold fields mined in California by early Spanish and Mexican miners before the 49ers came on the scene. Included are not only details on early mining methods in the area, production statistics and geological information, but also the location of the early gold mines that helped make California "The Golden State". Also included are details on the mining of other minerals such as silver, lead, zinc, manganese, tungsten, vanadium, asbestos, barite, borax, cement, clay, dolomite, fluospar, gem stones, graphite, marble, salines, petroleum, stronium, talc and others. **8.5" X 11"**, 116 ppgs. **Retail Price: $12.99**

Mines of Sierra County, California - Unavailable since 1920, this publication was originally compiled by the California State Mining Bureau and includes details on the gold mines of Sierra County, California. Also included are insights into the mineralization and other characteristics of this important mining region, as well as the location of historic gold mines. **8.5" X 11"**, 156 ppgs. **Retail Price: $19.99**

Mines of Plumas County, California - Unavailable since 1918, this publication was originally compiled by the California State Mining Bureau and includes details on the gold mines of Plumas County, California. Also included are insights into the mineralization and other characteristics of this important mining region, as well as the location of historic gold mines. **8.5" X 11"**, 200 ppgs. **Retail Price: $19.99**

Mines of El Dorado, Placer, Sacramento and Yuba Counties, California - Originally published in 1917, this important publication on California Mining has not been available for nearly a century. This publication includes important information on the early gold mines of El Dorado County, Placer County, Sacramento County and Yuba County, which were some of the first gold fields mined by the Forty-Niners during the California Gold Rush. Included are not only details on early mining methods in the area, production statistics and geological information, but also the location of the early gold mines that helped make California "The Golden State". Also included are insights into the early mining of chrome, copper and other minerals in this important mining area. **8.5" X 11"**, 204 ppgs. **Retail Price: $19.99**

Mines of Los Angeles, Orange and Riverside Counties, California - Originally published in 1917, this important publication on California Mining has not been available for nearly a century. This publication includes important information on the early gold mines of Los Angeles County, Orange County and Riverside County, which were some of the first gold fields mined in California by early Spanish and Mexican miners before the 49ers came on the scene. Included are not only details on early mining methods in the area, production statistics and geological information, but also the location of the early gold mines that helped make California "The Golden State". **8.5" X 11"**, 146 ppgs. **Retail Price: $12.99**

Mines of San Bernadino and Tulare Counties, California - Originally published in 1917, this important publication on California Mining has not been available for nearly a century. This publication includes important information on the early gold mines of San Bernadino and Tulare County, which were some of the first gold fields mined in California by early Spanish and Mexican miners before the 49ers came on the scene. Included are not only details on early mining methods in the area, production statistics and geological information, but also the location of the early gold mines that helped make California "The Golden State". Also included are details on the mining of other minerals such as copper, iron, lead, zinc, manganese, tungsten, vanadium, asbestos, barite, borax, cement, clay, dolomite, fluospar, gem stones, graphite, marble, salines, petroleum, stronium, talc and others. **8.5" X 11"**, 200 ppgs. **Retail Price: $19.99**

Chromite Mining in The Klamath Mountains of California and Oregon - Unavailable since 1919, this publication was originally compiled by J.S. Diller of the United States Department of Geological Survey and includes details on the chromite mines of this area of Northern California and Southern Oregon. Also included are insights into the mineralization and other characteristics of this important mining region, as well as the location of historic mines. Also included are insights into chromite mining in Eastern Oregon and Montana. **8.5" X 11"**, 98 ppgs. **Retail Price: $9.99**

Mines and Mining in Amador, Calaveras and Tuolumne Counties, California - Unavailable since 1915, this publication was originally compiled by William Tucker and includes details on the mines and mineral resources of this important California mining area. Included are details on the geology, history and important gold mines of the region, as well as insights into other local mineral resources such as asbestos, clay, copper, talc, limestone and others. Also included are insights into the mineralization and other characteristics of this important portion of California's Mother Lode mining region. **8.5" X 11", 198 ppgs. Retail Price: $14.99**

The Cerro Gordo Mining District of Inyo County California - Unavailable since 1963, this publication was originally compiled by the United States Department of Interior. Included are insights into the mineralization and other characteristics of this important mining region of Southern California. Topics include the mining of gold and silver in this important mining district in Inyo County, California, including details on the history, production and locations of the Cerro Gordo Mine, the Morning Star Mine, Estelle Tunnel, Charles Lease Tunnel, Ignacio, Hart, Crosscut Tunnel, Sunset, Upper Newtown, Newtown, Ella, Perseverance, Newsboy, Belmont and other silver and gold mines in the Cerro Gordo Mining District. This volume also includes important insights into the fossil record, geologic formations, faults and other aspects of economic geology in this California mining district. **8.5" X 11", 104 ppgs. Retail Price: $10.99**

Mining in Butte, Lassen, Modoc, Sutter and Tehama Counties of California - Unavailable since 1917, this publication was originally compiled by the United States Department of Interior. Included are insights into the mineralization and other characteristics of this important mining region of California. Topics include the mining of asbestos, chromite, gold, diamonds and manganese in Butte County, the mining of gold and copper in the Hayden Hill and Diamond Mountain mining districts of Lassen County, the mining of coal, salt, copper and gold in the High Grade and Winters mining districts of Modoc County, gold mining in Sutter County and the mining of gold, chromite, manganese and copper in Tehama County. This volume also includes the production records and locations of numerous mines in this important mining region. **8.5" X 11", 114 ppgs. Retail Price: $11.99**

Mines of Trinity County California - Originally published in 1965, this important publication on California Mining has not been available for nearly fifty years. This publication includes important information on mines and mining in Trinity County, California, as well insights into the mineralization and geology of this important mining area in Northern California. Included are extensive details on hardrock and placer gold mines and prospects, including charts showing the locations of these historic mines.. **8.5" X 11", 144 ppgs. Retail Price: $12.99**

Mines of Kern County California - Originally published in 1962, this important publication on California Mining has not been available for nearly fifty years. This publication includes important information on mines and mining in Kern County, California, as well insights into the mineralization and geology of this important mining area in California. Included are extensive details on hardrock and placer gold mines and prospects, including charts showing the locations of these historic mines. **8.5" X 11", 398 ppgs. Retail Price: $24.99**

Mines of Calaveras County California - Originally published in 1962, this important publication on California Mining has not been available for nearly fifty years. This publication includes important information on mines and mining in Calaveras County, California, as well insights into the mineralization and geology of this important mining area in Northern California. Included are extensive details on hardrock and placer gold mines and prospects, including charts showing the locations of these historic mines. **8.5" X 11", 236 ppgs. Retail Price: $19.99**

Lode Gold Mining in Grass Valley California - Unavailable since 1940, this publication was originally compiled by the United States Department of Interior. Included are insights into the gold mineralization and other characteristics of this important mining region of Nevada County, California. This volume also includes important insights into the geologic formations, faults and other aspects of economic geology in this California mining district. Of particular interest are the fine details on many hardrock gold mines in the area, including their locations, histories, development and mineralization. Some of the mines featured include the Gold Hill Mine, Massachusetts Hill, Boundary, Peabody, Golden Center, North Star, Omaha, Lone Jack, Homeward Bound, Hartery, Wisconsin, Allison Ranch, Phoenix, Kate Hayes, W.Y.O.D., Empire, Rich Hill, Daisy Hill, Orleans, Sultana, Centennial, Conlin, Ben Franklin, Crown Point and many others. **8.5" X 11", 148 ppgs. Retail Price: $12.99**

Lode Mining in the Alleghany District of Sierra County California - Unavailable since 1913, this publication was originally compiled by the United States Department of Interior. Included are insights into the mineralization and other characteristics of this important mining region of Sierra County. Included are details on the history, production and locations of numerous hardrock gold mines in this famous California area, including the Tightner Mine, Minnie D., Osceola, Eldorado, Twenty One, Sherman, Kenton, Oriental, Rainbow, Plumbago, Irelan, Gold Canyon, North Fork, Federal, Kate Hardy and others. This volume also includes important insights into the fossil record, geologic formations, faults and other aspects of economic geology in this California mining district. **8.5" X 11", 48 ppgs. Retail Price: $7.99**

Six Months In The Gold Mines During The California Gold Rush - Unavailable since 1850, this important work is a first hand account of one "49'ers" personal experience during the great California Gold Rush, shedding important light on one of the most exciting periods in the history of not only California, but also the world. Compiled from journals written between 1847 and 1849 by E. Gould Buffum, a native of New York, "Six Months In The Gold Mines During The California Gold Rush" offers a rare look into the day to day lives of the people who came to California to work in her gold mines when the state was still a great frontier. **8.5" X 11", 290 ppgs. Retail Price: $19.99**

Quartz Mines of the Grass Valley Mining District of California - Unavailable since 1867, this important publication has not been available since those days. This rare publication offers a short dissertation on the early hardrock mines in this important mining district in the California Mother Lode region between the 1850's and 1860's. Also included are hard to find details on the mineralization and locations of these mines, as well as how they were operated in those day. **8.5" X 11", 44 ppgs. Retail Price: $8.99**

Alaska Mining Books

Ore Deposits of the Willow Creek Mining District, Alaska - Unavailable since 1954, this hard to find publication includes valuable insights into the Willow Creek Mining District near Hatcher Pass in Alaska. The publication includes insights into the history, geology and locations of the well known mines in the area, including the Gold Cord, Independence, Fern, Mabel, Lonesome, Snowbird, Schroff-O'Neil, High Grade, Marion Twin, Thorpe, Webfoot, Kelly-Willow, Lane, Holland and others. **8.5" X 11", 96 ppgs. Retail Price: $9.99**

The Juneau Gold Belt of Alaska - Unavailable since 1906, this hard to find publication includes valuable insights into the gold mines around Juneau, Alaska. The publication includes important details into the history, geology and locations of the well known gold mines and prospects in the area, including those around Windham Bay, Holkham Bay, Port Snettisham, on Grindstone and Rhine Creeks, Gold Creek, Douglas Island, Salmon Creek, Lemon Creek, Nugget Creek, from the Mendenhall River to Berners Bay, McGinnis Creek, Montana Creek, Peterson Creek, Windfall Creek, the Eagle River, Yankee Basin, Yankee Curve, Kowee Creek and elsewhere. Not only are gold placer mines included, but also hardrock gold mines. **8.5" X 11", 224 ppgs. Retail Price: $19.99**

Arizona Mining Books

Mines and Mining in Northern Yuma County Arizona - Originally published in 1911, this important publication on Arizona Mining has not been available for over a hundred years. Included are rare insights into the gold, silver, copper and quicksilver mines of Yuma County, Arizona together with hard to find maps and photographs. Some of the mines and mining districts featured include the Planet Copper Mine, Mineral Hill, the Clara Consolidated Mine, Viati Mine, Copper Basin prospect, Bowman Mine, Quartz King, Billy Mack, Carnation, the Wardwell and Osbourne, Valensuella Copper, the Mariquita, Colonial Mine, the French American, the New York-Plomosa, Guadalupe, Lead Camp, Mudersbach Copper Camp, Yellow Bird, the Arizona Northern (Salome Strike), Bonanza (Harqua Hala), Golden Eagle, Hercules, Socorro and others. **8.5" X 11", 144 ppgs. Retail Price: $11.99**

The Aravaipa and Stanley Mining Districts of Graham County Arizona - Originally published in 1925, this important publication on Arizona Mining has not been available for nearly ninety years. Included are rare insights into the gold and silver mines of these two important mining districts, together with hard to find maps. **8.5" X 11", 140 ppgs. Retail Price: $11.99**

Gold in the Gold Basin and Lost Basin Mining Districts of Mohave County, Arizona - This volume contains rare insights into the geology and gold mineralization of the Gold Basin and Lost Basin Mining Districts of Mohave County, Arizona that will be of benefit to miners and prospectors. Also included is a significant body of information on the gold mines and prospects of this portion of Arizona. This volume is lavishly illustrated with rare photos and mining maps. **8.5" X 11", 188 ppgs. Retail Price: $19.99**

Mines of the Jerome and Bradshaw Mountains of Arizona - This important publication on Arizona Mining has not been available for ninety years. This volume contains rare insights into the geology and ore deposits of the Jerome and Bradshaw Mountains of Arizona that will be of benefit to miners and prospectors who work those areas. Included is a significant body of information on the mines and prospects of the Verde, Black Hills, Cherry Creek, Prescott, Walker, Groom Creek, Hassayampa, Bigbug, Turkey Creek, Agua Fria, Black Canyon, Peck, Tiger, Pine Grove, Bradshaw, Tintop, Humbug and Castle Creek Mining Districts. This volume is lavishly illustrated with rare photos and mining maps. **8.5" X 11", 218 ppgs. Retail Price: $19.99**

The Ajo Mining District of Pima County Arizona - This important publication on Arizona Mining has not been available for nearly seventy years. This volume contains rare insights into the geology and mineralization of the Ajo Mining District in Pima County, Arizona and in particular the famous New Cornelia Mine. **8.5" X 11", 126 ppgs. Retail Price: $11.99**

Mining in the Santa Rita and Patagonia Mountains of Arizona - Originally published in 1915, this important publication on Arizona Mining has not been available for nearly a century. Included are rare insights into hundreds of gold, silver, copper and other mines in this famous Arizona mining area. Details include the locations, geology, history, production and other facts of the mines of this region. **8.5" X 11", 394 ppgs. Retail Price: $24.99**

Mining in the Bisbee Quadrangle of Arizona - Originally published in 1906, this important publication on Arizona Mining has not been available for nearly a century. Included are rare insights into hundreds of gold, silver, copper and other mines in this famous Arizona mining area. Details include the locations, geology, history, production and other facts of the mines of this important mining region. **8.5" X 11", 188 ppgs. Retail Price: $14.99**

Montana Mining Books

A History of Butte Montana: The World's Greatest Mining Camp - First published in 1900 by H.C. Freeman, this important publication sheds a bright light on one of the most important mining areas in the history of The West. Together with his insights, as well as rare photographs of the periods, Harry Freeman describes Butte and its vicinity from its early beginnings, right up to its flush years when copper flowed from its mines like a river. At the time of publication, Butte, Montana was known worldwide as "The Richest Mining Spot On Earth" and produced not only vast amounts of copper, but also silver, gold and other metals from its mines. Freeman illustrates, with great detail, the most important mines in the vicinity of Butte, providing rare details on their owners, their history and most importantly, how the mines operated and how their treasures were extracted. Of particular interest are the dozens of rare photographs that depict mines such as the famous Anaconda, the Silver Bow, the Smoke House, Moose, Paulin, Buffalo, Little Minah, the Mountain Consolidated, West Greyrock, Cora, the Green Mountain, Diamond, Bell, Parnell, the Neversweat, Nipper, Original and many others. **8.5" X 11", 142 ppgs. Retail Price: $12.99**

The Butte Mining District of Montana - This important publication on Montana Mining has not been available for over a century. Included are rare insights into the gold, copper and silver mines of Butte, Montana together with hard to find maps and photographs. Some of the topics include the early history of gold, silver and copper mining in the Butte area, insight into the geology of its mining areas, the local distribution of gold, silver and copper ores, as well their composition and how to identify them. Also included are detailed facts about the mines in the Butte Mining District, including the famous Anaconda Mine, Gagnon, Parrot, Blue Vein, Moscow, Poulin, Stella, Buffalo, Green Mountain, Wake Up Jim, the Diamond-Bell Group, Mountain Consolidated, East Greyrock, West Greyrock, Snowball, Corra, Speculator, Adirondack, Miners Union, the Jessie-Edith May Group, Otisco, Iduna, Colorado, Lizzie, Cambers, Anderson, Hesperus, Preferencia and dozens of others. **8.5" X 11", 298 ppgs. Retail Price: $24.99**

Mines of the Helena Mining Region of Montana - This important publication on Montana Mining has not been available for over a century. Included are rare insights into the gold, copper and silver mines of the vicinity of Helena, Montana, including the Marysville Mining District, Elliston Mining District, Rimini Mining District, Helena Mining District, Clancy Mining District, Wickes Mining District, Boulder and Basin Mining Districts and the Elkhorn Mining District. Some of the topics include the early history of gold, silver and copper mining in the Helena area, insight into the geology of its mining areas, the local distribution of gold, silver and copper ores, as well their composition and how to identify them. Also included are detailed facts, history, geology and locations of over one hundred gold, silver and copper mines in the area . **8.5" X 11", 162 ppgs, Retail Price: $14.99**

Mines and Geology of the Garnet Range of Montana - This important publication on Montana Mining has not been available for over a century. Included are rare insights into the gold, copper and silver mines of the vicinity of this important mining area of Montana. Some of the topics include the early history of gold, silver and copper mining in the Garnet Mountains, insight into the geology of its mining areas, the local distribution of gold, silver and copper ores, as well their composition and how to identify them. Also included are detailed facts, history, geology and locations of numerous gold, silver and copper mines in the area . **8.5" X 11", 100 ppgs, Retail Price: $11.99**

Mines and Geology of the Philipsburg Quadrangle of Montana - This important publication on Montana Mining has not been available for over a century. Included are rare insights into the gold, copper and silver mines of the vicinity of this important mining area of Montana. Some of the topics include the early history of gold, silver and copper mining in the Philipsburg Quadrangle, insight into the geology of its mining areas, the local distribution of gold, silver and copper ores, as well their composition and how to identify them. Also included are detailed facts, history, geology and locations of over one hundred gold, silver and copper mines in the area **8.5" X 11", 290 ppgs, Retail Price: $24.99**

Geology of the Marysville Mining District of Montana - Included are rare insights into the mining geology of the Marysville Mining District. Some of the topics include the early history of gold, silver and copper mining in the area, insight into the geology of its mining areas, the local distribution of gold, silver and copper ores, as well their composition and how to identify them. Also included are detailed facts, history, geology and locations of gold, silver and copper mines in the area **8.5" X 11", 198 ppgs, Retail Price: $19.99**

The Geology and Mines of Northern Idaho and North Western Montana

See listing under Idaho.

Nevada Mining Books

The Bull Frog Mining District of Nevada - Unavailable since 1910, this publication was originally compiled by the United States Department of Interior. This volume also includes important insights into the geologic formations, faults and other aspects of economic geology in this Nevada mining district. Of particular interest are the fine details on many mines in the area, including their locations, histories, development and mineralization. Some of the mines featured include the National Bank Mine, Providence, Gibraltor, Tramps, Denver, Original Bullfrog, Gold Bar, Mayflower, Homestake-King and other mines and prospects. **8.5″ X 11″, 152 ppgs, Retail Price: $14.99**

History of the Comstock Lode - Unavailable since 1876, this publication was originally released by John Wiley & Sons. This volume also includes important insights into the famous Comstock Lode of Nevada that represented the first major silver discovery in the United States. During its spectacular run, the Comstock produced over 192 million ounces of silver and 8.2 million ounces of gold. Not only did the Comstock result in one of the largest mining rushes in history and yield immense fortunes for its owners, but it made important contributions to the development of the State of Nevada, as well as neighboring California. Included here are important details on not only the early development and history of the Comstock, but also rare early insight into its mines, ore and its geology.**8.5″ X 11″, 244 ppgs, Retail Price: $19.99**

Colorado Mining Books

Ores of The Leadville Mining District - Unavailable since 1926, this publication was originally compiled by the United States Department of Interior. This volume also includes important insights into the ores and mineralization of the Leadville Mining District in Colorado. Topics include historic ore prospecting methods, local geology, insights into ore veins and stockworks, the local trend and distribution of ore channels, reverse faults, shattered rock above replacement ore bodies, mineral enrichment in oxidized and sulphide zones and more. **8.5″ X 11″, 66 ppgs, Retail Price: $8.99**

Mining in Colorado - Unavailable since 1926, this publication was originally compiled by the United States Department of Interior. This volume also includes important insights into the mining history of Colorado from its early beginnings in the 1850's right up to the mid 1920's. Not only is Colorado's gold mining heritage included, but also its silver, copper, lead and zinc mining industry. Each mining area is treated separately, detailing the development of Colorado's mines on a county by county basis. **8.5″ X 11″, 284 ppgs, Retail Price: $19.99**

Gold Mining in Gilpin County Colorado - Unavailable since 1876, this publication was originally compiled by the Register Steam Printing House of Central City, Colorado. A rare glimpse at the gold mining history and early mines of Gilpin County, Colorado from their first discovery in the 1850's up to the "flush years" of the mid 1870's. Of particular interest is the history of the discovery of gold in Gilpin County and details about the men who made those first strikes. Special focus is given to the early gold mines and first mining districts of the area, many of which are not detailed in other books on Colorado's gold mining history. **8.5″ X 11″, 156 ppgs, Retail Price: $12.99**

Mining in the Gold Brick Mining District of Colorado - Important insights into the history of the Gold Brick Mining District, as well as its local geography and economic geology. Also included are the histories and locations of historic mines in this important Colorado Mining District, including the Cortland, Carter, Raymond, Gold Links, Sacramento, Bassick, Sandy Hook, Chronicle, Grand Prize, Chloride, Granite Mountain, Lucille, Gray Mountain, Hilltop, Maggie Mitchell, Silver Islet, Revenue, Roosevelt, Carbonate King and others. In addition to hardrock mining, are also included are details on gold placer mining in this portion of Colorado. **8.5″ X 11″, 140 ppgs, Retail Price: $12.99**

Washington Mining Books

The Republic Mining District of Washington - Unavailable since 1910, this important publication was originally published by the Washington Geologic Survey and has been unavailable for a century. Topics include the geology, rock formations and the formation of ore deposits in this important mining area of Washington State. Also included are hard to find details on the geology, history and locations of dozens of mines in the area. Some of the mines featured include the New Republic Mine, Ben Hur, Morning Glory, the South Republic Mine, Quilp, Surprise, Black Tail, Lone Pine, San Poil, Mountain Lion, Tom Thumb, Elcaliph and many others. **8.5″ X 11″, 94 ppgs, Retail Price: $10.99**

Wyoming Mining Books

Mining in the Laramie Basin of Wyoming - Unavailable since 1909, this publication was originally compiled by the United States Department of Interior. Also included are insights into the mineralization and other characteristics of this important mining region, especially in regards to coal, limestone, gypsum, bentonite clay, cement, sand, clay and copper. **8.5" X 11", 104 ppgs, Retail Price: $11.99**

New Mexico Mining Books

The Mogollon Mining District of New Mexico - Unavailable since 1927, this important publication was originally published by the US Department of Interior and has been unavailable for 80 years. Topics include the geology, rock formations and the formation of ore deposits in this important mining area in New Mexico. Of particular focus is information on the history and production of the ore deposits in this area, their form and structure, vein filling, their paragenesis, origins and ore shoots, as well as oxidation and supergene enrichment. Also included are hard to find details, including the descriptions and locations of numerous gold, silver and other types of mines, including the Eureka, Pacific, South Alpine, Great Western, Enterprise, Buffalo, Mountain View, Floride, Gold Dust, Last Chance, Deadwood, Confidence, Maud S., Deep Down, Little Fanney, Trilby, Johnson, Alberta, Comet, Golden Eagle, Cooney, Queen, the Iron Crown, Eberle, Clifton, Andrew Jackson mine, Mascot and others. **8.5" X 11", 144 ppgs, Retail Price: $12.99**

The Percha Mining District of Kingston New Mexico - Unavailable since 1883, this important publication was originally published by the Kingston Tribune and has been unavailable for over one hundred and thirty five years. Having been written during the earliest years of gold and silver mining in the Percha Mining District, unlike other books on the subject, this work offers the unique perspective of having actually been written while the early mining history of this area was still being made. In fact, the work was written so early in the development of this area that many of the notable mines in the Percha District were less than a few years old and were still being operated by their original discoverers with the same enthusiasm as when they were first located. Included are hard to find details on the very earliest gold and silver mines of this important mining district near Kingston in Sierra County, New Mexico. **8.5" X 11", 68 ppgs, Retail Price: $9.99**

East Coast Mining Books

The Gold Fields of the Southern Appalachians - Unavailable since 1895, this important publication was originally published by the US Department of Interior and has been unavailable for nearly 120 years. Topics include the geology, rock formations and the formation of ore deposits in this important mining area of the American South. Of particular focus is information on the history and statistics of the ore deposits in this area, their form and structure and veins. Also included are details on the placer gold deposits of the region. The gold fields of the Georgian Belt, Carolinian Belt and the South Mountain Mining District of North Carolina are all treated in descriptive detail. Included are hard to find details, including the descriptions and locations of numerous gold mines in Georgia, North Carolina and elsewhere in the American South. Also included are details on the gold belts of the British Maritime Provinces and the Green Mountains. **8.5" X 11", 104 ppgs, Retail Price: $9.99**

Gold Rush Tales Series

Millions in Siskiyou County Gold - In this first volume of the "Gold Rush Tales" series, leading mining historian and editor Kerby Jackson, introduces us to the story of how millions of dollars worth of gold was discovered in Siskiyou County during the California Gold Rush. Lavishly illustrated with photos from the 19th Century, this hard to find information was first published in 1897 and sheds important light onto the gold rush era in Siskiyou County, California and the experiences of the men who dug for the gold and actually found it. **8.5" X 11", 82 ppgs, Retail Price: $9.99**

The California Rand in the Days of '49 - In this second volume of the "Gold Rush Tales" series, leading mining historian and editor Kerby Jackson, introduces us to four tales from the California Gold Rush. Lavishly illustrated with photos from the 19th Century, this hard to find information was first published in 1890's and includes the stories of "California's Rand", details about Chinese miners, how one early miner named Baker struck it rich and also the story of Alphonzo Bowers, who invented the first hydraulic gold dredge. **8.5" X 11", 54 ppgs, Retail Price: $9.99**

More Mining Books

Prospecting and Developing A Small Mine - Topics covered include the classification of varying ores, how to take a proper ore sample, the proper reduction of ore samples, alluvial sampling, how to understand geology as it is applied to prospecting and mining, prospecting procedures, methods of ore treatment, the application of drilling and blasting in a small mine and other topics that the small scale miner will find of benefit. **8.5" X 11", 112 ppgs, Retail Price: $11.99**

Timbering For Small Underground Mines - Topics covered include the selection of caps and posts, the treatment of mine timbers, how to install mine timbers, repairing damaged timbers, use of drift supports, headboards, squeeze sets, ore chute construction, mine cribbing, square set timbering methods, the use of steel and concrete sets and other topics that the small underground miner will find of benefit. This volume also includes twenty eight illustrations depicting the proper construction of mine timbering and support systems that greatly enhance the practical usability of the information contained in this small book. 8.5" X 11", 88 ppgs. Retail Price: $10.99

Timbering and Mining - A classic mining publication on Hard Rock Mining by W.H. Storms. Unavailable since 1909, this rare publication provides an in depth look at American methods of underground mine timbering and mining methods. Topics include the selection and preservation of mine timbers, drifting and drift sets, driving in running ground, structural steel in mine workings, timbering drifts in gravel mines, timbering methods for driving shafts, positioning drill holes in shafts, timbering stations at shafts, drainage, mining large ore bodies by means of open cuts or by the "Glory Hole" system, stoping out ore in flat or low lying veins, use of the "Caving System", stoping in swelling ground, how to stope out large ore bodies, Square Set timbering on the Comstock and its modifications by California miners, the construction of ore chutes, stoping ore bodies by use of the "Block System", how to work dangerous ground, information on the "Delprat System" of stoping without mine timbers, construction and use of headframes and much more. This volume provides a reference into not only practical methods of mining and timbering that may be employed in narrow vein mining by small miners today, but also rare insights into how mines were being worked at the turn of the 19th Century. 8.5" X 11", 288 ppgs. Retail Price: $24.99

A Study of Ore Deposits For The Practical Miner - Mining historian Kerby Jackson introduces us to a classic mining publication on ore deposits by J.P. Wallace. First published in 1908, it has been unavailable for over a century. Included are important insights into the properties of minerals and their identification, on the occurrence and origin of gold, on gold alloys, insights into gold bearing sulfides such as pyrites and arsenopyrites, on gold bearing vanadium, gold and silver tellurides, lead and mercury tellurides, on silver ores, platinum and iridium, mercury ores, copper ores, lead ores, zinc ores, iron ores, chromium ores, manganese ores, nickel ores, tin ores, tungsten ores and others. Also included are facts regarding rock forming minerals, their composition and occurrences, on igneous, sedimentary, metamorphic and intrusive rocks, as well as how they are geologically disturbed by dikes, flows and faults, as well as the effects of these geologic actions and why they are important to the miner. Written specifically with the common miner and prospector in mind, the book will help to unlock the earth's hidden wealth for you and is written in a simple and concise language that anyone can understand. 8.5" X 11", 366 ppgs. Retail Price: $24.99

Mine Drainage - Unavailable since 1896, this rare publication provides an in depth look at American methods of underground mine drainage and mining pump systems. This volume provides a reference into not only practical methods of mining drainage that may be employed in narrow vein mining by small miners today, but also rare insights into how mines were being worked at the turn of the 19th Century. 8.5" X 11", 218 ppgs. Retail Price: $24.99

Fire Assaying Gold, Silver and Lead Ores - Unavailable since 1907, this important publication was originally published by the Mining and Scientific Press and was designed to introduce miners and prospectors of gold, silver and lead to the art of fire assaying. Topics include the fire assaying of ores and products containing gold, silver and lead; the sampling and preparation of ore for an assay; care of the assay office, assay furnaces; crucibles and scorifiers; assay balances; metallic ores; scorification assays; cupelling; parting' crucible assays, the roasting of ores and more. This classic provides a time honored method of assaying put forward in a clear, concise and easy to understand language that will make it a benefit to even beginners. 8.5" X 11", 96 ppgs. Retail Price: $11.99

Methods of Mine Timbering - Originally published in 1896, this important publication on mining engineering has not been available for nearly a century. Included are rare insights into historical methods of timbering structural support that were used in underground metal mines during the California that still have a practical application for the small scale hardrock miner of today. 8.5" X 11", 94 ppgs. Retail Price: $10.99

The Enrichment of Copper Sulfide Ores - First published in 1913, it has been unavailable for over a century. Topics include the definition and types of ore enrichment, the oxidation of copper ores, the precipitation of metallic sulfides. Also included are the results of dozens of lab experiments pertaining to the enrichment of sulfide ores that will be of interest to the practical hard rock mine operator in his efforts to release the metallic bounty from his mine's ore. 8.5" X 11", 92 ppgs. Retail Price: $9.99

A Study of Magmatic Sulfide Ores - Unavailable since 1914, this rare publication provides an in depth look at magmatic sulfide ores. Some of the topics included are the definition and classification of magmatic ores, descriptions of some magmatic sulfide ore deposits known at the time of publication including copper and nickel bearing pyrrohitic ore bodies, chalcopyrite-bornite deposits, pyritic deposits, magnetite-ileminite deposits, chromite deposits and magmatic iron ore deposits. Also included are details on how to recognize these types of ore deposits while prospecting for valuable hardrock minerals. 8.5" X 11", 138 ppgs. Retail Price: $11.99

<u>The Cyanide Process of Gold Recovery</u> - Unavailable since 1894 and released under the name "The Cyanide Process: Its Practical Application and Economical Results", this rare publication provides an in depth look at the early use of cyanide leaching for gold recovery from hardrock mine ores. This volume provides a reference into the early development and use of cyanide leaching to recover gold. **8.5" X 11", 162 ppgs. Retail Price: $14.99**

<u>California Gold Milling Practices</u> - Unavailable since 1895 and released under the name "California Gold Practices", this rare publication provides an in depth look at early methods of milling used to reduce gold ores in California during the late 19th century. This volume provides a reference into the early development and use of milling equipment during the earliest years of the California Gold Rush up to the age of the Industrial Revolution. Much of the information still applies today and will be of use to small scale miners engaging in hardrock mining. **8.5" X 11", 104 ppgs. Retail Price: $10.99**